Titanic

The History and Legacy of the World's Most Famous Ship

(The Original News Reporting of the Sinking of the Titanic)

Lester Lake

Published By **John Kembrey**

Lester Lake

All Rights Reserved

Titanic: The History and Legacy of the World's Most Famous Ship (The Original News Reporting of the Sinking of the Titanic)

ISBN 978-1-77485-758-8

No part of this guidebook shall be reproduced in any form without permission in writing from the publisher except in the case of brief quotations embodied in critical articles or reviews.

Legal & Disclaimer

The information contained in this ebook is not designed to replace or take the place of any form of medicine or professional medical advice. The information in this ebook has been provided for educational & entertainment purposes only.

The information contained in this book has been compiled from sources deemed reliable, and it is accurate to the best of the Author's knowledge; however, the Author cannot guarantee its accuracy and validity and cannot be held liable for any errors or omissions. Changes are periodically made to this book. You must consult your doctor or get professional medical advice before using any of the suggested remedies, techniques, or information in this book.

Upon using the information contained in this book, you agree to hold harmless the Author from and against any damages, costs, and expenses, including any legal fees potentially resulting from the application of any of the information provided by this guide. This disclaimer applies to any damages or injury caused by the use and application, whether directly or indirectly, of any advice or information presented, whether for breach of contract, tort, negligence, personal injury, criminal intent, or under any other cause of action.

You agree to accept all risks of using the information presented inside this book. You need to consult a professional medical practitioner in order to ensure you are both able and healthy enough to participate in this program.

TABLE OF CONTENTS

Introduction 1

Chapter 1: The History Of Rms Titanic 4

Chapter 2: Features, Dimensions And Layout 16

Chapter 3: Safety Protection 33

Chapter 4: Titanic Sets Sailing 44

Chapter 5: Tragic Events Strike The Titanic 53

Chapter 6: The Aftermath Of Sinking 78

Chapter 7: The Survivors Of The Disaster 90

Chapter 8: Preparations For The "Monster" Type Of Ships 103

Chapter 9: Putting Together The Stories Of Survivors 126

Chapter 10: The Survivors Go Home 156

Chapter 11: Titanic Found At Long Last 176

Conclusion 183

Introduction

Fast. The world at the start of the 20th century was a fast one. The industrial revolution was changing the world of Great Britain and the United States. Everywhere you went there were steel structures soaring out of the ground. Everything was being constructed faster. The messages were moving faster. Cities were expanding quicker: New York City gathered more than half a million new residents between 1890 and 1900. The same time it was estimated that the U.S. population grew by 14 million 21, or 21 percent.

The automobile was new and although they were speedy they weren't speedy enough for everyone, especially those who were rich, which were becoming richer each day. Pittsburgh industrialist Henry Clay Frick was tired of his horse-less carriage in 1910. The reason? The congestion that kept the horse's power. He changed to air travel by having his chauffeur buy planes and lessons in the air, then traveling between Manhattan to Massachusetts during weekends.

Speed was among the main tenets on the basis of which The Titanic was built. The times demanded and revered speed, and the high stakes business deals that were conducted across the Atlantic required speed.

The second main principle that was shaping The Titanic was this new transatlantic mood. Henry James is famous for the theme of this novel as well as an emerging new trend. In addition, a plethora of immigrants were fleeing hardships of all kinds throughout England as well as other European countries, and were scavenging the market for hundreds of massive ocean liners that were being constructed in the quickest time feasible.

The third element was the act of ostentation. The ship was the first to have an indoor pool. It had telephones before many homes had. Its passengers who weren't "huddled crowds" mentioned in the caption of the Statue of Liberty were wealthy in ways that had not been possible for 30 or 40 years earlier and a terrifying sort of new wealth that was made possible by steel, automobiles and railroads. The Titanic fit in with these types of people due to its speed, fast in a manner that was truly amazing. It was a technological marvel similar to the modern industrialists were creating and selling. However, it also provided them with luxurious amenities such as roast ducklings and foie gras steam baths as well as tennis courts. Class stratification was soaring upwards as the heights of a New York City high rise and those who were in the dizzy heights needed keep a constant reminder of their loftiness.

In this sense, The Titanic was an symbol of its time. It was massive, sturdy and heavy, as well as, sure enough, it was fast. It shouldn't have subjected its passengers with the more obvious segregation of social groups. It was, however it was unsinkable.

Chapter 1: The History Of Rms Titanic

The 103rd anniversary of the tragic events of the sinking of the RMS Titanic, readers will be informed of the events that took place prior to the catastrophe and the primary causes that led to the catastrophe. Additionally, readers will also gain understanding of the consequences of the tragedy and the grief of the survivors and their families.

The tragedy caused by the sinking RMS Titanic dates back to more than a century ago, the it is a reminiscence that sends chills down the spines of relatives of the victims from the disaster. The tragic tale is an motivation that has drawn a huge viewers due to the powerful combination of irony, tragedy, and love.

The events of the tragic incident are permanently remembered by the citizens of America. United States, which excites those who study and are interested to know more about the true motive that led to the tragic event of April 2012 that saw the sinking of the RMS Titanic. Each new study uncovers an entirely new aspect of the tale. If you talk to relatives of survivors, each person you talk to will reveal a new detail.

The author has attempted to bring together a wealth of information about the tragedy, which was obtained through interactions with a variety of individuals who are either directly or distantly connected to the victims of the tragic event.

You might be wondering why this tragic tale is so captivating to a reader and the reason is that the events that transpired preceding the tragic accident are intended to give readers an historical perspective and convey the entire incident in a fun way. First-person and historical evidence can also give information about the historical background of the building of the Olympic cruise ship. The in-depth information about the vessel's construction transports readers on a journey to a world of wonder in which you'll feel the euphoria in your own way.

The concept of this amazing ship was conceived during the era called"the Gilded Age, a period which saw advancements and changes in the technology and culture industry. White Star Line designed the luxurious ship in accordance with Olympic standards. It was one of the initial three luxury ships built in this class.

The fascinating story of RMS Titanic dates back to the early hours of the 15th of April 1912 in which the British passenger vessel collided with an iceberg before being submerged into the vast ocean in the North Atlantic Ocean. In 1912, the RMS Titanic had set sailing for the first time. the point of boarding is Southampton located in The United Kingdom, and the ship was headed towards New York City in the United States.

Furthermore, the tragic event caused the deaths of more and over 1500 people, including crew members as well as passengers. This is the primary reason the accident has been described among the most devastating and most fatal maritime catastrophes that occurred on a luxury commercial ship in the present.

One of the largest ships in the maritime sector and Titanic was one of the largest ships in the maritime industry. RMS Titanic set afloat as one of three ocean liners designed by White Star Line under the category of Olympic-standard luxury ships. The designers of this ocean liner were an entire team of naval architects from Belfast such as Thomas Andrews. It was the RMS Titanic was a great design and was the first step towards the creation of Wolff and Harland shipyard. Tragically, the tragedy also killed the naval architect Thomas Andrews. This ocean-liner had been ready for her first cruise, with the intention to provide an unforgettable cruise experience for crew members along with the 2224 passengers aboard.

In the beginning in the early 20th century Belfast was growing with the development of industry and, eventually, it was an industrial center which was home to more than 3 lakh residents which is nearing the number of 4 lakh. People in Belfast sought jobs in various industries areas like linen, shipbuilding, and engineering.

Shipyards in Wolff and Harland were technically designed to serve as the manufacturing site for more than 70 vessels for marine use from the company White Star Line. The company has developed well-known vessels that meet Olympic standards like Titanic, Britannic, Olympic, and Titanic. All three ocean liners of the Olympic class were constructed with a distinctive style in the years 1908-2014. Today two incredible twin cranes built within the same shipyards under the names of Samson and Goliath remain high, guarding Belfast. Belfast.

Edward Smith, commander of the RMS Titanic, was travelling in the ship's inaugural voyage with a group of the wealthiest people from various parts of the world. A number of immigrants had arrived to Ireland, Great Britain, Scandinavia and other European nations in an effort to discover their new lives in the area that was North America.

This ocean-liner controlled using marconigrams, which are an instrument like the wireless telegraph invented by Guglielmo Marconi. The captain sent instructions to the ships of other vessels in the event an accident occurred. For example, the news about the tragedy was relayed to the other ocean liner that was the Olympic by way of the marconigram. The message read "Eleven pm New York Time Titanic Sending Out Signals of Distress. Titanic Answered his Calls. Titanic responds and gives me his location 41.46 The message reads N 50 14, W and states "We have smashed an Ice Berg". Our Distance from Titanic 505 miles"

While RMS Titanic comprised of essential safety features, in accordance with the safety standards set by the US government, such as watertight compartments, as well as doors that were watertight that controlled by remotes however, the tragedy took place in the real world. The Titanic was not equipped with sufficient lifeboats to accommodate every passenger on board that day Furthermore, the vessel was in compliance with safety regulations that were deemed to be unnecessary by the regulators for marine operations.

RMS Titanic had the facility of just a couple of lifeboats and the total number of passengers who traveled in its first voyage was nearly twice that amount, and just one third of the passengers could access the lifeboat after disaster struck the liner's ocean. Titanic was able to carry only the capacity of 1,178 lifeboats, over half of the passengers onboard and one third of her total capacity.

The architects claimed they had constructed the most secure ship with the name of RMS Titanic, such that it is the top vessel when it comes to safety standards.

However, do you think of that the Titanic as the most secure vessel in the world since there were no lifeboats aboard the ship which meant that it could cater to the requirements of only half of the people traveling on board?

There was a misunderstanding in the belief of the fact that materials utilized to construct the ocean liner gave strength to the vessel, so that it was referred to as being 'unsinkable'. It is believed that the ship was robust and stable. Lifeboats were only required if the ship sinks , and also as a way to save the survivors. Furthermore, the lifeboats occupied a sufficient room on the deck of the vessel so they were not as numerous. In addition, the architects never imagined extremely confident in the strength and endurance of the vessel. Nobody could have imagined that while building the vessel that it would witness its completion in its maiden journey itself.

The RMS Titanic witnessed the darkest night of the year on April 14, 1912, at 11:40 pm after it struck an iceberg, following four days of enjoying an easy ride. The captain of the ship who was a lucky survivor states that the impact of the collision sounded similar to the decomposition of the calico. The collision ended in death and killed numerous people as icy water started to seep into the liner of ocean.

It was apparent that a large number of passengers would not have access to the safety features provided through the lifeboat. Even those who were provided with life jackets weren't able to make it through the night as a human being will not be able to live in temperatures below 4 degrees below the point of freezing.

The passengers began to panic as the front of the Ocean Liner began sinking further. One lucky survivor was John Thayer. John Thayer saw the ship sinking because he was in the lifeboat. He says, "We could see groups of about 15 hundred passengers still on board that were clinging to the ship in clusters or groups like bees swarming; but then they fell in masses or pairs, or even singly in the huge after section that was the vessel, 200 fifty feet began to rise up to the sky until it was at a sixty-five or seventy degrees angle."

After the collision, ship sank slowly over the course of two hours and forty minutes.

The birth of RMS Titanic

The style of ocean-liner RMS Titanic was a result of the growing competition among luxurious ships in 1907.

A lot of emphasis was put on the creation of a luxury vessel that was massive rather than a vessel with a fast speed. The director in charge, Joseph Bruce Ismay, was keen to build the biggest ocean liner in the time.

The first ship constructed as a luxury ship included The Olympic as RMS Titanic was the second in the line of product. The building of the Olympic was completed on the 16th of December 1908. Then came the building of RMS Titanic; the project began in less than the span of three months i.e. March 31st 1909. The amazing appearance of the ship was to be acknowledged as an engineering marvel in that time; RMS Titanic topped the charts in the categories of speed, size, and luxurious ocean linesrs.

Within three years from the start of the construction work, RMS Titanic was ready to sail in the most impassioned cruise of the history of the past three decades. The first voyage of the luxurious ocean liner was planned for Southampton which would finish with a stop in New York. People from all categories of life stepped aboard the ship, silent film actors, immigrants, as well as schoolteachers were eager to participate.

After five days of an easy journey the ocean liner moved quickly across the Atlantic Ocean. Based on reports of other ocean liner regarding icebergs, Capt. Edward Smith, the commander of RMS Titanic, prepared the navigation route in a manner that would avoid blocking. However, it's generally believed that no one could ever challenge their fate or fate.

While sailing across the tranquil sea, under a blue sky with no moon, and in a frigid temperature, it was difficult to discern the iceberg, and then accidentally the catastrophe struck RMS Titanic.

Chapter 2: Features, Dimensions And Layout

Have you ever considered what the reasons RMS Titanic is described as one of the most stunning luxurious ships in the world? The first reason is that the ship is unique in its design and is focused on luxury facilities and size , instead of quick movement. Furthermore, this vessel featured unique attributes sizes, dimensions, and layout which make it unique.

The Shipbuilders Council of America praises the distinctive style that is Titanic as RMS Titanic as, "unrivalled magnitude and beauty .... in its magnitude and beauty." outstanding outcome is beyond anything else."

The style that was the design of RMS Titanic had a capacity of carrying more than 3000 passengers in total. It could accommodate a crew of 860 and around 2300 passengers.

The passengers on Titanic's RMS Titanic were grouped into three categories: 1st 3rd and 4th classes with capacity of 689, 674 and 1026 passengers within the travel category of their choice.

The deck of the ship consists of ten parts, including the deck of the boat (A) as well as the higher deck (F) promenade deck (B) middle deck (G) and the bridge deck (C) lower deck(C), shelter deck an orlop deck for saloons and the tank's top.

The decks of the ship are comprises three distinct parts comprising The fore area, the amidships and aft. Fore is situated on the ship's front side, while amidship is the center of the vessel and the aft situated on the rear of the vessel.

The total mass of this cruise ship was 46,328 pounds; it had a length of 883 feet and covered beams up at 93 feet. The cruising speed of RMS Titanic was 22.5 knots and it was able to displace the equivalent of 66,000 tons of water. The maximum depth of the vessel was 44 feet. The ship was equipped with four smokestacks which each measured 62 feet in length and with a diameter of 22 feet.

The rudder on the ship had a maximum height of 78 feet. It was divided into six equal pieces with the total weight was around 101 tons. The ship was guided by three anchors, weighing approximately 31 tons total. It also included three propellers, with the three outer propellers on each side of the vessel with 23 feet of diameter while the propeller in the middle, with 17 feet of diameter.

The other parts that make up Titanic's other components of RMS Titanic include one turbine engine two steam engines that operate on four furnaces, 159 cylinders, 15 bulkheads, 29 boilers 20 lifeboats, as well as 16 compartments that are watertight.

The lifeboats were kept on the deck of the boat and were used in emergency situations. The ship also included an Poop deck (in the present, it's known in the modern era as the toilet). This deck could be visible because it was on the roof of cabins to the rear. To go from one deck to another, passengers took the elevator, also called the 'Grand Staircase'.

The most frequent areas for accommodations for passengers as well as areas that were accessible to the public were the Shelter deck Promenade deck Bridge deck the saloon deck and the deck below. Promenade deck, as well as the boat decks did not extend across the entire ship. The lengths of the Bridge decks, the poop deck along with the forecastle deck measured 1,282 feet, 550 feet and 106 feet respectively.

The ship also provided modern recreation options for its passengers. Facilities included Turkish bath as well as a swimming pool, gym as well as squash courts.

Facilities for passengers in 1st Class

On board, passengers had access to the reception area as well as a dining saloon, lounge smoking room, restaurant, writing -

reading room with palm courts, as well as cafes with verandas.

The Grand Staircase

It is a gem on the crown of RMS Titanic. The 60-foot grand staircase is a stunning collection of the finest glass, wrought iron along with polished wood. The staircase's design is influenced by the classic William and Mary design of the 17th century. It is constructed under an overhanging dome that creates stunning optical illusions due to natural light throughout the day. In the middle of the design is the huge wall has been cut out that is the wall clock. The majority of passengers descend the grand staircase to access the dining area at the top of the line, or they choose to use the elevators. The light fixture for the cherub near the at the top of the stairs reveals the distinctive style of the wood carved which supports the clock on the wall.

The female passengers on the 1st class mainly utilized the reading-writing area. Large windows were erected on the side of the room that overlooked the balcony of the promenade.

It was a great location for those who wanted to sip a drink smoking a puff. Non-smokers could visit the room to look at the glass art on windows which depicted the various ships created in the name of White Star Line as well as the unique elegance of ports around the globe.

The room also takes guests to the verandah, which is a view of the palm courts and the forward part of the Promenade.

The trip was a great value for the money paid by first-class passengers due to the luxury amenities on offer. Its Cafe Parisien was a fantastic dining spot on the ship due to the fact that the design for the café was comparable to the modern bouquet cafes that are found in Paris.

First-class passengers were able to stay in a hotel with all the luxury amenities. Additionally, they had access to Lounge and the deck of Promenade. They could gather in this section of the ship, or enjoy a conversation in private while enjoying delicious beverages and food. The Lounge was decorated with a stunning design as was the style used by Louis XV. French monarch, Louis XV. It is decorated with a portrait "Approach to the New World" The original design by Norman Wilkinson.

The Reception Room takes passengers into the vessel's Dining Room. This Dining Room sports a Jacobean style of architecture with a white hue. It spans across 114 feet. the dining room can accommodate 532 guests in one sitting.

The layout of RMS Titanic arranged for the addition of 39 suites. i.e. 30 suites with private bathrooms were situated on Bridge deck while the remaining nine suites were located on the deck of shelter. Each suite had an attached bathroom with a bedroom as well as 5 rooms i.e. 2 wardrobes, 2 bedrooms and a bathroom.

First-class passengers were also able to access the A-la-carte restaurant, that served a variety of the finest food items from all over the globe were displayed on platters. The restaurant could accommodate anywhere between 2 and 8 diners at a table. Its architecture bears a striking likeness to the classic French architectural style that was popular under the reign of Louis XIV. The walls and ceiling of the restaurant had an elegant look because of the elegant moldings and decorations. Lamps and chandeliers hanging from the central panel and silk curtains made plenty of space for first-class guests. Live entertainment was offered as an orchestra performing at an elevated stage in the restaurant. It is said that you will are more satisfied with your meal when you are listening to soft music.

A huge dining hall stretched over 1000 square. meters and could serve 554 people at once. A total of 115 tables, each able to accommodate 12 people at once was the layout of the dining room. The interior of the room was created with wooden panels, which were painted white in hue. Floor tiles constructed of linoleum colored blue with a distinctive pattern that alternated between red and yellow. The exquisite design of portholes of the dining saloon and the glass windows that had an inner lining constructed from lead created the impression that the passengers were dining along the beach. The cooking of meals for the space was carried out in the adjoining kitchen, where meals were served to passengers traveling on the 2nd class too.

Facilities for passengers in 2nd Class

Seven decks were accessible to passengers on the 2nd class RMS Titanic. The majority of the time, passengers walked through the Dining Room to access into the Smoking Room. The library had similar facilities similar to those provided in the premier library. Mahogany furniture was an added element of the beautiful style of the library, and added to its uniqueness. The library had a massive bookcase, which was situated just in front of the bulkhead. Silk curtains were hung on the massive windows to give the royal look. The Wilton carpet's material created an inviting warm ambience inside the library.

The accommodation for passengers of second class was well-worth the money. The ship offered rooms with 2 or 4 berths , which were constructed inside cabin walls. The walls were painted in white enamel The rooms were able to accommodate up to 550 people and were furnished with fashionable furniture made of mahogany. While curtains were available for every bed, privacy was a main concern for the second-class passengers.

The Dining Room was at 71 feet long and could accommodate 2400 guests simultaneously. The elegant dining room is due to the pivoted sidelights which were housed in wooden panels that were made from oak. The music played by the piano provided a tranquil atmosphere for dining guests.

The staterooms' design was similar to the typical cabins found on the vessel's first deck.

Facilities for 3rd Class Passengers

It is evident that the accommodations as well as the leisure facilities available to passengers on the 3rd class RMS Titanic was a bit lower than those offered for first-class travel as well as second-class travel. The third category of amenities was also known as'steerage that accommodated 1,000 passengers in total. The smallest accommodations available included rooms with between two and six beds. Onboard cabins amounted to 84 cabins that had two-berths.

The passengers were from different ethnic groups and regions. A large portion of passengers were Irish, British, or Scandinavian. The immigrants who came from Sweden, Finland, Croatia, Bulgaria, Lebanon, Hong Kong, Russia, and Syria were on board the RMS Titanic with a hope of discovering a new and more fulfilling life on the other side of North America. The diverse group of passengers aboard included solo travelers and single mothers with kids and large families.

The room's size was a signpost to the type of passenger on that portion on the boat. The separation between the vessel's distinct sections also showed the division between classes in this time.

The Turkish bath for 3rd class baths were smaller than the one accessible to first class passengers. Bathrooms were accessible through a shared basis. two bathtubs could be used by numerous passengers. The number of users sometimes more than 700 people. Separate bathtubs were accessible for women and men. Since many passengers couldn't use to the Turkish bathtub, the majority made use of the facilities of the galley.

Sleeping arrangements were designed with bunk beds. Six persons were accommodated in the cabin's narrow.

In contrast to a standard dormitory, the layout that the bedrooms were different. The rooms were designed as an individual closed cabin however, the purpose behind designing such a space was to create the privacy of the cabin could accommodate up to six people the passengers were required to share their cabins with other guests.

The General Room was the principal meeting place for passengers. It was located on the starboard side of the ship's liner. It was used as a of a recreation room and lounge and even the nursery.

The wall surface were painted with white enamel, paired with a pine hues. The space was furnished with furniture made of teakwood. Upholstery was absent from the room for hygiene reasons. This does not mean the interiors were dark and the walls were decorated with posters relating to the diverse vessels built by the White Star Line Company as and the numerous ports that the company operates.

Smoke Room Smoke Room was a visual pleasure for male guests. They had access to a private bar and the space was designed for spittoons to dispose of the tobacco chewed. Oak panels were affixed to the wall area and the space was furnished with comfy furniture constructed of teakwood.

It was apparent by the appearance of the third-class ship that it could accommodate only migrants. Because people were moving towards North America with a hope of a better future and better life, they left their country with their entire savings. The goal of the space was to inspire an aura of confidence that would allow the people who were emigrating to begin their new life content.

The dining area was situated on the middle deck which was a space that stretched over 100 feet, and covering all the length of ocean liner. In the average of 470 people, the ship fed at the same time. The ship's kitchen and the pantry was located behind the dining room. There was only one meal served for passengers. The standard menu included soup, a combination of two or three vegetables roast pork biscuits, pudding and biscuits. Tea was served to passengers at the end of the afternoon, usually at 3 or 4pm together with beef and biscuits. Evening coffee was served along by biscuits and a cup of soup.

The passengers were required to organize themselves for entertainment and leisure. Kids sometimes took part in an unplanned dance to entertain passengers.

The passengers had a thorough health check-up prior to their entry on the ship in order to identify any illnesses, diseases or lice.

The piano was set in an upright position, and it was adjacent to the wall on the side in the area. Studies have shown that this piano was bought from a music store since it was a replica of the model that was manufactured in accordance with the standards of the industry.

A photo from the Olympic revealed that the music sheets were left open with the top of the piano was is propped up.

The unfortunate fact is that passengers in this class suffered the most victimized by the tragic loss of life; many passengers lost their lives in the tragedy. There are many reasons that are responsible for the deaths of so many passengers in third class which will be discussed in the subsequent chapters.

Facilities for Crew Members

The crew comprised 322 stewards, and 23 female employees. Assisting 57 people with different tasks isn't something that is easy to do however, the members of the crew did a great job in performing various functions and services, including dining salons within every class, cabins and public rooms and even recreation services. The crew comprised 62 members in the kitchen as well as the galley, which included cooks and cooks, chefs, bakers dishwashers and butchers. Only 13 members of the crew survived the tragic incident. The other staff members comprised 24 engineers and boilermakers, and 10 electricians.

The crew's accommodation was designed so that the crew wouldn't be able interact with passengers in person at any point during the trip. They were required to communicate using the aid from the marconigram.

Staff members from the engine room were based on the starboard area on the front of the vessel. The rooms for engines were situated on the lower, upper and middle the saloon decks. The crew members were able to access the engine room as well as the boiler through two spiral staircases.

The passengers were aiming to find an opportunity to find a new hope in their lives. Little did they realize they are likely to die during the journey.

Chapter 3: Safety Protection

Over a century ago in the past, more than a century ago, the RMS Titanic witnessed a tragic ending, as she crashed into an iceberg that was floating in the North Atlantic Ocean, and killed more than 1500 people on her first journey. Instead of reaching the prestigious destinations in New York, the ocean liner sank into the grave of the oceans deep in 1912. The tragic incident has turned into an act of caution for the public , warning their fears about the dangers of human insecurity. The hopes were destroyed and the scars left by the tragic incident are visible.

Security Specifications of RMS Titanic

1. One of the biggest issues with the design of the Royal Mail Ship Titanic is the absence of a sufficient number of lifeboats aboard the vessel. The ship's designers were proud of the fact they used the most effective materials for the construction of the ship, consequently, it was branded with the title "Unsinkable". This is why they didn't consider it necessary to have

sufficient lifeboats for the ship to aid all passengers in the event of an emergency. The vessel actually had just a fraction of that number of lifeboats when compared to the capacities of the liner.

Two elements are the main reason behind the popularity of these techniques of shipbuilding used by a variety of manufacturers. First, ship builders were utilizing outdated maritime safety rules that did not include the requirement of lifeboats on a vessel that was as massive as Titanic. RMS Titanic. In actual fact, Titanic had arranged for more lifeboats than was stipulated by guidelines for maritime safety.

Another feature that this model had was the dimensions that the lifeboat. The lifeboat took up a significant amount of space within the ship and the designers were keen to leave the deck uncluttered. They also included just a handful of lifeboats to be used in emergencies.

The disaster became a catastrophe as a large portion of lifeboats were ripped off of the ship after Titanic struck the Iceberg. Additionally there were lifeboats that did not have the capacity to save the lives of people as the crew were not experienced in managing the lifeboats and helping the people to wear it in a proper way.

The worst part was that there were only two lifeboats remaining in the ship, even though 17 people were aboard. In the beginning of the design process for the RMS Titanic it was tested that one lifeboat could be sufficient to hold 70 people at a time. But, during the time of testing the technology was completely unusable. In the aftermath of the incident, everyone was hurrying to get a seat on the lifeboat. However, this did little to help. Additionally, a exercise or demonstration using the lifeboat scheduled on 14th April be canceled because crew and passengers were keen to attend a large numbers.

It is true that nobody can predict what your future will bring you.

2. Watertight Compartments: The designers were confident in their original design of compartments that were watertight in Titanic's RMS Titanic. It was not a surprise that the compartments would be the way for a major tragic event in the history of modern times.

The basic design of the ship was divided into 16 compartments, which were operated by doors that were watertight made of metal. The hull features a perforated trap inside each compartment to trap the water and prevent the entrance of water throughout the ship.

In the worst-case scenario the compartments could help the vessel to sink into the water at a very slow pace which will allow rapid evacuation of the passengers the event an emergency. The problem was the lack of a roof for the compartments which didn't contribute an additional watertight characteristics that the ship. Therefore, when the ship hit the iceberg the hull that was present in the first 6 watertight compartments failed to stop the ingress from water in the vessel. In the end, the bulkhead began to fill up with water which inundated the compartment adjacent, which in turn it led in the chain reaction which eventually caused the vessel to sink. Thus, the ocean liner was able to sink faster than the designers had anticipated it to sink.

3. Marconigram/Wireless radio: In 1912, the usage of a marconigram to communicate to the Captain of a ship with his passengers was a contemporary idea. It was an excellent source to earn money when wealthy passengers would use the radio system that was wireless during their voyage to send or receive messages.

Additionally it was able to cover a considerable distance, and even crew members proved to be efficient using Morse codes as a way of communicating.

In all likelihood, human error could prove the most efficient technology in complete shambles and result in a tragic accident.

The team that was operating the radio's wireless communication was engaged in numerous discussions in conversation with Captain Edward Smith; several warnings regarding icebergs were issued the RMS Titanic that was ignored by the Titanic crew. Therefore, Captain Smith was not aware of the alerts, and continued to sail the ocean liner across the most deadly ocean.

The crew members took care of the passenger requirements and considered the warnings from the iceberg to be insignificant. They did not pay attention to the warnings. This could have prevented the catastrophe since another vessel "Californian" was close proximity to offer immediate assistance. While Titanic was sinking, RMS Titanic was sinking the wireless radio system on the Californian was either not being operated or the signals were shut off.

4. Buoyancy Rings - A formal complaint was not filed regarding the lack of life vests to the passengers on board. The vest

that was worn was made of a strong material, including cork and canvas. The ocean liner was been arranged with buoyancy rings. In total, the ship had 48 buoyancy rings on board. The purpose was to serve as being an attraction piece instead of a security device.

In the event that the sinking Titanic was to have been at a location close to the Equator and the buoyancy rings, as well as the life jacket would have been beneficial. A large number of passengers died before they drowned due to suffering from hypothermia i.e. the body's heat is produced quickly due to the extremely low temperatures in the outside surroundings. The temperature of the sea water was approximately 1degC If a person is exposed to that temperature for more than 15 minutes, is likely to die instantly.

Safety lessons

Following the loss of RMS Titanic, ship builders have begun paying more attention to regulations governing safety on the sea. Additionally, the policies of the government concerning maritime safety have been modified to safeguard the lives of those who travel on luxury vessels.

Certain researchers have concluded that a lot of experts were not in agreement with the most modern design of RMS Titanic.

The first safety lapse was that the luxurious ships had special features such as the thick bottom, watertight bulkheadsand doors with electric seals that were watertight and these characteristics caused the vessels to be uninkable. The watertight compartments in the bulkhead allowed for the movement through the water passage from one compartment to another, and a minor defect in the design could aid in the passage of water through the compartments, eventually reaching the whole ship that eventually occurred.

Additionally, if Titanic had been equipped with enough lifeboats, not just 16 collapsibles, many more lives could be saved. The ship was carrying more than 300 passengers on board , which included passengers and crew members and crew members, the safety measures must have been able to accommodate everyone. Even ifyou think about the maximum capacity of each lifeboat it is only able to save 1/3 of the passengers onboard in an emergency.

The crew was also not efficient when it came to handling the lifeboats and their life jackets. The study revealed that four lifeboats had not been filled at their full capacity, and Some of them were had been filled to 50% of their total capacity. The maximum capacity of a lifeboat is to hold 40 passengers, but one lifeboat could only hold 12 people. Furthermore, the training drill for using the lifeboat was cancelled as speculation suggests that the drill may have saved lives.

The fourth thing we learn from the tragic incident of sinking RMS Titanic is that the ocean liner didn't have the right tools and safety equipment. The crew was not equipped with a have enough flashlights and binoculars and had just 37 seconds for responding prior to the disaster. The lack of time cost many lives which could have been spared.

The second major lesson is the fact that the liner didn't have any backup plans in case of emergency. A second ship was located close quarters, the vessel was not able to receive immediate aid due to the lack of knowledge of the of the crew who were on the other vessel. It was later discovered that around 700 passengers did not receive any assistance in the span of about three hours, resulting in their suffering fatal injuries or their death.

Numerous agencies have been created in the wake of the tragedy to develop guidelines for maritime safety. In the case of The International Ice patrol was established in January 1914. A International Convention was organized on November 12, 1913 to debate the idea of the safety in Life at Sea (SOLA) as a resounding lesson from the tragedy that struck RMS Titanic. In the United States, the US Coast Guard has established an agency that is responsible for monitoring and reporting on the location of the most prominent icebergs along the northern portion of the Atlantic Ocean in order to assist ships to navigate safely and avoid icebergs during their transatlantic journey.

The last but not last, it has created awareness among the population about the maritime regulations that are imposed to ensure safety. Regularly revised the maritime safety rules is observed to ensure an enjoyable journey for passengers. Nearly 1500 passengers were killed during the catastrophe.

Today the passengers are taught to use lifeboats and life jackets in the event in an emergency. Safety drills are offered all over the world for using the safety equipment. Standards for industry are set to ensure the safety of ships with a particular focus on emergency evacuations and the training of crew members in handling the equipment.

Chapter 4: Titanic Sets Sailing

Timeline

The development status of the date of RMS Titanic

April 1 2012, 2012 Sea trials of RMS Titanic delayed due to bad weather

April 02 1912, 1912 Sea trials for RMS Titanic begin at 06:00 hours; the sea trials end at 20:00 hours and RMS Titanic is ready to sail off from the docks in Southampton

April 4 1912 RMS Titanic arrives in Southampton just after midnight.

April 10 1912 April 10, 1912 Captain William James Pirrie, Chairman, Harland & Wolff is not able to embark on RMS Titanic due to ill health. At 1730 hours, RMS Titanic reaches Cherbourg in France.

April 11 1912. RMS Titanic reaches Queenstown in Ireland and departs in the morning at 13:00 hours to arrive at New York City on time.

April 14th 1912 RMS Titanic strikes against an Iceberg at 23:40 hours.

15 April 1912, the ship begins sinking at 02:20 am Another ship, the Carpathia is able to save the first survivors in the lifeboats.

April 18th, 1912 survivors are able to get ashore from the Titanic at 21:00 hrs , when the Carpathia is at New York

The first journey of RMS Titanic dates back to April 10, 1912 which was the day she left the docks at Southampton port to head toward New York, travelling with over 3000 passengers as well as crew members.

There was a long delay when she launched her first journey because of a collision between an of three luxurious vessels that was the Olympic which was in September 1911, together with HMS Hawke; moreover, an engine had gone missing from the vessel. The ship's manufacturers wanted the Olympic to launch before the Titanic.

After the successful trials in the oceans in Ireland, Titanic travelled a short distance to the port that are located in Southampton located in England from which she would begin her first voyage. Unfortunately, it was to be the very first and final voyage for the renowned high-end ocean liner.

The ship arrived at the point of boarding at Southampton with only two weeks left to go out and set sail, it put a huge pressure on ship builders to convert into a Irish ship into an British Royal Mail Steamer that will be a symbol for the beauty and grace that is inherent to.

The ship was outfitted with the most desirable things like food, linen, furniture and interior decor, etc. to create a warm and comfortable atmosphere to passengers. Furthermore, the best skilled people were picked to be the personnel members who had been trained to master the particular skill sets.

Captain of the vessel Capt. Edward James Smith was the ideal choice to lead through the RMS Titanic through the vast expanse of the North Atlantic Ocean to reach New York; his stature and media presence and a seasoned crew were an ideal fit for the shipbuilding company, White Star Lines.

Another issue that delayed the time in the launch for the liner's ocean voyage was lack of coal caused by strikes on coal; RMS Titanic was capable of up to 600 tons of coal per day. The issue was resolved temporarily using coal sourced from vessels like The Oceanic as well as the Adriatic to provide the required quantity of coal needed for the first voyage of Titanic, the liner for oceans.

On April 10th, 1912 the day that RMS Titanic left the port of Southampton in the afternoon. The captain and the ship's builders realize they would would have its first incident within a brief time span The ship was involved in minor collision with the vessel named New York. The collision was not as destructive than the plunge into the enormous expanse of North Atlantic Ocean. It was nevertheless shocking and was an alarm for the ship's crew as well as the builders. The next day, she travelled to Cherbourg, France, and Queensland, Ireland to collect more passengers in the 1320 number , along with 907 crew members.

If you think you feel that RMS Titanic had a smooth voyage right from the moment when it first began its voyage but you're not so sure. The beginning of her inaugural voyage was not particularly exciting since it was traveling slow. As time passed, the ship began to speed up It traveled 352 miles and 519 miles in addition to 546 miles on the first the, second and third day of the journey, respectively.

You may not be conscious that a fire broke through a coalbunker prior to the ship was set to sail. The coalbunkers were prone to fire. an issue that was common due to the combustion in coal dust. Small sparks could ignite fire throughout all bunkers.

RMS Titanic's Route RMS Titanic

The innovations in technology used to create the RMS Titanic assigned the term "unsinkable" to the vessel. 14 people aboarded the ship in Belfast when they watched the RMS Titanic set sail on her first voyage. The sea trials of the vessel were conducted by an entire crew of 400. They quit the ship when the trials had concluded in Southampton. But, some people on the ship remained aboard and fell victim to the most tragic maritime incident in history.

Around 922 passengers boarded the RMS Titanic from Southampton; 24 passengers departed in Cherbourg and 8 others were able to leave Titanic in Ireland.

274 people travelled on the Titanic at Cherbourg and became those who died as they were traveling to North America. The passengers on the RMS Titanic included the richest citizens of Europe and also immigrants. 120 passengers embarked aboard the RMS Titanic from Queenstown in Ireland. Over 2000 passengers were aboard the Titanic for its first voyage. The

clock struck 11.40 pm, and it was the 14th of April 1912 in which the liner escaped collision with an Iceberg. It was travelling 400 miles further the ship was away of Cape Race in Newfoundland when ultimately tragedy struck the ship. The ship was evacuated in a chaotic manner. conducted as the ocean liner remained floating for about two hours and forty-five minutes after it hit the Iceberg. The date was April 15th, 1912. in the early hours of dawn, exact date was 2.20 am, when the massive luxury vessel sank under the ocean's waters.

Sail over the Atlantic Ocean

Initial plans required that the RMS Titanic to reach New York Pier 54 on April 17. The ocean liner crossed the oceans of Ireland following the arrival of passengers on the vessel from Queenstown. The ship traveled for about 55 nautical miles, after the direction of navigators to travel further by 1620 nautical miles in the circle of the North Atlantic Ocean in order to reach Newfoundland which was the location from which ships traveling west changed direction.

The ocean liner set sail for about 1177 miles. She arrived at Nantucket Shoals Light following which she was struck by an Iceberg. The final phase of her journey it would have taken over 222 miles to reach Ambrose Light and the journey was to end in the harbor of New York City.

In the first phase of her first voyage, RMS Titanic sailed smoothly without any issues. As the ship left Ireland the ship was confronted with the possibility of stormy and cloudy weather. A headwind was making trouble for the sailing of the luxury vessel. It was mild temperature on the 13th of April 1912. However, on April 14th, 1912 it became cold and fierce winds were blowing. Sea water rose to 8 feet, or 2.4 meters. However, the weather grew comfortable and remained stable throughout the day. The skies cleared in the evening.

Other ships sent signal warnings for RMS Titanic notifying the crew to beware of icebergs in Newfoundland but the crew members did not heed these warnings and the vessel was moving at a rapid speed. In those days the normal practice of the maritime industry permitted ships to travel at full speed. However, more importance was given to timekeeping . As consequently, advisories were put on the bridges to assist ships with warnings regarding icebergs as and any assistance maritime that was needed by any ship traversing the Atlantic Ocean.

Chapter 5: Tragic Events Strike The Titanic

It was the 14th of April 1912 and, for the passengers of the Titanic the day was turning into a dark, cold evening illuminated by stars. On its way towards New York, the Titanic was speeding along at a high rate as it was approaching Newfoundland which was located just to the south of Labrador. While most ships tried to stay clear of the area because of the icebergs and frigid temperatures that could threaten safety but the Titanic was in a time-bound schedule and had to make it to the States as fast as it could. Therefore, the ship continued to travel to avoid danger even though many of the passengers aboard heard rumors about Captain Smith was in a dispute over the ship's course in a meeting with Mr. Bruce Ismay, the managing director of White Star Line. Actually Captain Smith was planning to change the direction of the ship and move further south after he heard about the risky floating ice in the area, however

Mr. Ismay was determined to stick the current schedule. Unfortunately Ismay prevailed. Ismay was able to prevail and the plan was the same despite the fact to have been the case that Titanic had received 7 warnings regarding icebergs in the time during the course of. After the decision was made that each warning issued from the Titanic's radio operator, Jack Phillips and Harold Bride was ignored, and the ship continued to slam into the iceberg zone. Captain Smith attempted to limit anxiety by hiding the details from his crew members, and not divulging the actual dangers of the warnings until after they had been delivered. Unfortunately, Captain Smith's decision to minimize the risk may have contributed to Titanic's inexperience when the ship later struck the Iceberg.

After the crew had learned about the risks posed through the S.S. Baltic and the S.S. Californian, Second Officer Lightoller advised the lookouts to watch for Icebergs. However, identifying icebergs in the dark of night was a challenging task, particularly since the most dangerous icebergs like the one that Titanic struck, were entirely submerged. This is why it's not surprising that the first officer who was directing the ship's navigation from the deck was unable to spot the iceberg in the distance and stopped the Titanic from getting the time it needed to alter its direction. At the point that watchman Frederick Fleet spotted the iceberg at 11:40pm on in the evening on April 14, it had been early for Titanic. When Fleet noticed the black outline in the water, he dialed the alarm three times and called the bridge immediately, notifying all the other crew members to respond. As efforts were underway to salvage the situation first officer William Murdoch attempted to stop the ship and move to the left so as to avoid the frozen iceberg. However, the iceberg was extremely formidable under the surface, as well as being thirty meters taller than upper deck of the vessel.

In the evening of 11:45 pm of April 14th, 1912 the Titanic was sunk by its starboard side into an enormous Iceberg that tore away nearly half the vessel and taking out the bulkheads nearly completely. When the iceberg hit the water began to rise immediately towards the forward part of the vessel, reaching 14 feet at 11:50 at night. Although some ice blocks were thrown onto the deck when the ship collided with the iceberg injury was hidden below the surface. Sadly, when the bulkheads were being removed as well as unable defend the ship in the way they were meant to, the vessel began sinking more and more quickly. Because the bulkheads of the ship were constructed in a peculiar way and the bulkhead was not attached to the deck aboveit, the water quickly filled up the gap between the bulkheads and deck until the ship was filled. After that, when Captain Joseph Boxhall went to check the lower levels of the ship and revealed the volume of water pouring into the ship captain Smith along with Thomas Andrews, the ship's builder, were aware that it was in danger. The Titanic was designed to float in the event that four of the ship's compartments were filledup, however five of them were flooded. It was thought by the engineer to release steam immediately to keep the ship from collapsing however whether the ship could be able to withstand the wreck was another story. The Titanic was almost certain to sink and all that was to be left for crew members accomplish was to bring the passengers to safety. And, of course, continue to communicate emergency messages all the time the Titanic kept its head above water as they only had less than a few hours to go before the ship could sink.

As the crew began delivering passengers to lifeboats, radio operator Jack Phillips and Harold Bride issued emergency messages, requesting assistance from any ship which may be in the vicinity. They initially broadcast an emergency call-out C.Q.D .--"Come Quick Danger"--and later, they began to send the brand new urgent message S.O.S .--"Save Our Ship"--making the Titanic the first ship to be the first to utilize the new emergency message. The later documentation revealed that S.S. Birma, a Russian liner located nearby was the first to receive the S.O.S. radio-telegram sent by the Titanic at 11:45 pm , and continued to receive this message for the duration of 14th and 15th April. The message in the distress call was "we have hit an iceberg that is sinking rapidly, help us." It also read "S.O.S. to M.G.Y.," with M.G.Y. as the codename for the Titanic. The official documentation puts the Titanic at the latitude of 41.46 North and longitude 50.14 W at the time that the S.O.S. was delivered.

At the beginning Phillips and Bride laughed about the possible risk of water that was iceberg-infested, Phillips telling Bride that the next time he went to "see his first Iceberg" and that "Americans would be happy because they all love Ice in their drinks," the laughter did not last for long. After they finally received the RMS Carpathia finally responded to the message, Phillips and Bride understood the inevitable that the Titanic and the other passengers on the ship, wouldn't endure the collision with the iceberg. The reality of the incident resulted in the Carpathia was almost in the wrong place to receive the message of emergency from the Titanic that arrived just at a time when Carpathian Radio operating Harold Cottam usually turned in to bed. Due to the fact that he was late and listening to his music while he was getting ready for bed, Cottam managed to catch the emergency message and promptly called the captain of the incident. Although that the Captain of the Carpathia and Captain Rostron had already settled into bed at night Cottam awakened him, and told him of the situation with the Titanic. While both individuals were reeling from the shock of what had happened--isn't the Titanic supposed to be unsinkable? -Captain Rostron immediately reacted to the situation and promptly switched the ship to toward the Titanic. Despite his swift reaction and willingness to propel his ship to its fullest to assist but the Carpathia was unable to arrive at the Titanic for an additional four hours. The Titanic was, however, just had two hours before sinking. In a flash, Phillips and Bride had the lives of Titanic passengers being based on their accomplishments and as they began searching for a closer ship that could help but failed to locate any. In addition, the growing disturbance and noise on the vessel was making it extremely difficult for them to perform their duties, yet they continued to send emergency messages until the final.

In the meantime, passengers on the Titanic had heard the powerful sounds of the ship hitting the iceberg. Many were in a state of panic, even though the crew attempted to confine them to their rooms initially to prevent chaos. Although the power went out briefly, causing anxiety and causing some passengers to be curious however, the crew managed to stabilize the situation temporarily and ensure the safety of the passengers. Even with the harrowing sound of steam being released and the quick actions of crew members the passengers were not allowed to ascend above decks, mainly because it was very cold. So, it took several minutes before they were aware of the crash that killed a person and the true conditions. When word of the crash spread and the crew started the process of removing the ship, a lot of people on the ship did not think that the scenario was real. The Titanic was invincible; it was impossible that running into an iceberg could sink the entire ship, or it seemed to them. In spite of their disbelief they started to plan to leave the ship should it be necessary. The reality of their predicament was only getting acknowledged.

The Titanic was a horror of a failure to prepare to deal with an eventual emergency. As passengers began to plan for a disaster, the deficiency of emergency equipment and the lack of training was shockingly obvious. First of all, the majority of passengers aboard the ship were unaware of the location of their lifebelts and it was not essential to provide instructions for emergencies when they boarded the "unsinkable" Titanic.

Additionally, a lot of guests were not equipped with lifebelts at all or had one malfunctioning or was not accessible. After the lifebelts were found and the passengers were seated on the main deck to discover that there weren't enough lifeboats to hold the entire group. There were 2200 passengers aboard however, there were only lifeboats to accommodate 1178 passengers. Whatever way they dealt with it out, one thing was that There was no guarantee that everyone would make it through the sinking of Titanic.

Initial, the passengers' evacuation was relatively smooth crew members opened blankets in barrels, and then distributed them as swiftly as was possible as they could, and passengers from first-class cabins were able to get up to the deck. However, when it took third and second class passengers a bit longer to get to the deck on their own, which caused some to be anxious and be concerned that they would not get out on sufficient time. The crew was able to keep order and nearly all of them made it to the top the deck. As the passengers began to gather but the crew was faced with a brand completely new and incredibly frustrating scenario as a lot of passengers' doubts made them unable to get on the lifeboats, insisting to remain on the ship. Although the crew tried try to convince the passengers that it was essential to leave the ship however, many believed that the Titanic was going to survive the disaster and refused to get on the lifeboats. Why should they put their lives in danger on a boat that was not tested in freezing waters if they could trust the security and safety provided by the Titanic? This meant that a number of the first vessels that were launched before they had reached their full capacity, and were filled to only half or a quarter of the way. In one instance a lifeboat designed for 70 people was left empty with just 12. Skepticism and inability to effectively utilize the limited resources available is among the most tragic events of the Titanic's sinking.

The crew was sent to set up the lifeboats and bring the passengers aboard at around 12:05 am on April 15, the children and women began to board the lifeboats at 12:25 am. Around this time that the Carpathia got word of the Titanic's distress prompting them to turn around and assist, even though they just 58 miles away. The first lifeboat launched at 12:45 am, even though it was carrying only 28 people, when it could have had 65. At the same time the Titanic was launching it's first rocket of distress although no ships were nearby enough to observe the launch. The Titanic launched seven more rockets before night was finished and there was no one other than the Carpathia helping it.

The lifeboats began to leave to be filled with children and women, as the truth of their circumstances became evident and more problems were identified. With the Titanic in a position of extreme danger and the deck's slope increasing every second crew members were no longer able to access the lifeboats located on the top of the Titanic's deck, which put a lot of the few lifeboats that were on the ship completely out of service. In addition, because the Titanic had not conducted an inspection of safety before departing port, it was not discovered until the iceberg struck that the majority of the Titanic's emergency gear was damaged or was missing. In addition to the lifebelts that some passengers weren't found, many lifeboats were inoperable or not functioning due to different reasons. A lot of lifeboats were fed improperly, which prevented them from lowering the proper way, sometimes making them crash across the side of the vessel before it crashed in the freezing water. These lifeboats plunged to the bottom, threatening the lives of passengers who were on board as well as the other vessels in the vicinity which were sometimes being struck by the falling vessels. Furthermore certain lifeboats themselves were incorrect and some compartments were collapsed or compartments damaged. This led to passengers being more reluctant to leave the ship, convinced it wasn't worth the risk of putting their lives in a dangerous lifeboat. However, as the Titanic became more prominent but the need to get a lifeboat on board whether it was erroneous or not increased until the passengers were no longer given a option. You could either take your chance in a lifeboat or sink.

Sadly, as the risk of remaining aboard the Titanic becoming more apparent the desire to take lifeboats that were not reliable grew exponentially. Although the initial phases of leaving the ship had been relatively peaceful, the passengers were almost still or in whispered whispers, the panic grew when the number of lifeboats dwindled. Soon, fathers and husbands forced the children and wives onto the boats, with women crying when they left. A few, knowing that the likelihood that they'd never meet their loved ones again started crying and screaming when the lifeboats left with the sound drowning out the sound from the sinking Titanic. Some passengers later shared tales of the final moments, reminiscing about the generosity of a few or the bravery of other passengers. A woman named Molly Brown, was one of the first-class passengers aboard the third lifeboat that helped save a man's life by covering the man in her jacket and kept him warm on the lifeboat until Carpathia arrived. Another woman named Mrs. Ida Straus, gave her spot in the lifeboat and stayed with her husband, stating that "we've shared our lives and will pass away together." In another instance the sailor gave his lifebelt to Minnie Coutts who was a third-class participant and the mother of two children, who did not have enough life belts for her and her kids. After she sincerely thanked him and thanked him, the sailor smiled and added, "If the boat goes down, I'll be there to remember you!"

However, certain passengers were less brave and their actions caused members of the team to adopt a stronger position to ensure that as many people off the vessel as they could. As the numbers grew larger and more passengers tried to board lifeboats already full The crew was armed and threatening the crowd with threats to follow instructions or face punishment for their inconsiderateness. In one incident one man disguised as a woman attempted to board a lifeboat only to have a member of the crew find the man as a threat to kill him in case the man didn't take off his boat. In another incident, the sailor pointed his gun at a boy of a certain age who was hiding with children in a lifeboat insisting that he dress as a man and take off his boat so the younger child could be in his place. The boy agreed. After the final lifeboat was brought in to be filled, the crew created a strong, arm-in-arm barrier against the crowd, and allowed only the most number of children and women onto the vessel to keep it from being overcrowded. The actions of the crew members of courage, however ended up costing them their lives and the majority of the crew perished along together with the ship.

While the lifeboats were filled and sent off there was a final spark of hope was spotted before the ship completely sank. The reason for this hope was finding a vessel just 6-10 miles away that was close enough to passengers on board the Titanic to see it in the fading light. Unfortunately, while they lit up firecrackers as well as continued to relay emergency messages to everyone who was in the area the ship finally went in the opposite direction and disappeared into darkness. The speculation surrounding the mysterious ship and its motives for choosing not to aid the Titanic has led to several possible scenarios. There is a possibility, as some have suggested that the vessel was a smaller fishing boat unlawfully entering the waters, which is the reason it appeared suddenly and then departed without providing any assistance. The most likely explanation is that the vessel is one of the S.S. California, and even though it was close by but it was not equipped with the necessary equipment for long distance radio and thus was not capable of receiving or transmitting long distance radio communications. This could explain why it did not receive the Titanic's distress signals, and more importantly that it misinterpreted Titanic's distress signals. As per the team members on the S.S. California, the rockets seemed to be fireworks from afar, and, given the Titanic's reputation and its status as a newly-minted luxurious vessel they were unsure to be concerned about these rockets. This incident led people to realize that it was that all ships be equipped with a long-distance telegram, as well as hiring sufficient crew members to allow this radio system to be operated continuously.

Finally, as the two remaining lifeboats were beginning to overflow, Captain Smith advised the crew to "do their best for children and women" and to then save themselves whenever they were able to. Then, as the last lifeboat had left at 2:05 am, with more than 1500 people still in the boat the Captain broadcast his last radio broadcast at 2:17am "Every one for his own." Then that platform on the ship grew ever steeper which made it more difficult for the people to stand upright.

The furnishings in the room fell into a loud smash, a number of passengers were tossed out of the boat, crashing into the freezing waters below. There was a lot of panic as people began searching looking for options to get out of the water, while others simply jumped overboard in hopes of swimming to an emergency lifeboat or another source. Unfortunately, the majority of people who were affected suffered the same situation, when their bodies eventually began to freeze submerged for a while in the freezing water.

Others, conscious that they were not likely to be prospects of salvation, believed that it was more important to face death in a dignified manner and accept the fate they were handed. They included people like Benjamin Guggenheim, a first-class passenger who wore a suit and declared his intention to live just as was a gentleman. The orchestra, helmed by Wallace Hartley, also stayed at their posts, performing as passengers climbed aboard the lifeboats, until every possibility for a way out was taken. Even when Hartley advised the musicians to help themselves the group refused, and decided to remain together, and played one last song before the ship sinks.

In the final hours of the Titanic on the cold morning of the middle of April, 1912, the darkness fell as the ship was sinking, sending out stars and over the sky an unsettling black. A massive wave crashed onto the Titanic's deck, dragging the ship into water's murky depths as it began sinking more and more quickly. A loud thud the ship broke into two pieces, raising expectations one final time that the smaller fragment would be able to stay floating. However, their hopes were unanswered. Despite the stern was able to settle till it leveled and the water continued to flood the vessel. The stern started to tilt again until it the ship was totally upside down, throwing everyone on board into the water which froze them to death. After that, the vessel was completely submerged with a huge sound, drowning out the sound of screaming and crying against the dark sky. When 2:20 a.m. came around on the frigid and cold morning of the 15th April 1912 The "Queen of the Ocean" was gone.

If you were in the water, there was nothing to do. Even if they could locate something to float, they were likely to die of hypothermia in the shortest time of. For the remaining survivors and those who were lucky enough to be in the lifeboats, the odds of survival were low. The lifeboats themselves weren't prepared for a true emergency--none were equipped with light sources or food or water. And in the dark it was difficult to know if someone was on the way to help them. While many of the lifeboats tried to stay to rescue survivors who made it out alive, the crews of the vessels quickly realized that they must get far from the scene as they could in order to stay clear of being submerged by the sinking vessel. After that, they were left with no idea of what to do as no one could tell whether a ship was on the way to rescue them, which meant they had to remain in the vicinity or if they would be better off finding an area of land independently. However, the lifeboats were only equipped with the oars. This wouldn't bring them anywhere fast enough to allow them to be saved. As the darkness grew and the silence grew over the sea The survivors slowed down. A few cried out in hysterics, however, for the majority the entire group was stunned to silence. With the exception of some who were hopeful, the majority of people had to accept themselves to the fate they were in, believing they had managed to escape from a sinking ship only to suffer the consequences of hunger and hypothermia. If another ship had not been able to rescue them many survivors would have died in the night.

The morning finally came bright and clear and the survivors realized to their astonishment, to their dismay, that they were floating in an ocean that was smothered with layers of ice. But their dismay didn't last longas with the dawn's light came the sighting that there were rockets visible in distant areas, indicating that a ship must be on its way. It was around 3:00 am. Around 4:10 am, Carpathia had made an ecstatic effort to assist the Titanic after receiving the emergency call it had arrived. When the ship snatched up the lifeboats and put people aboard the vessel, the friendly people on board the Carpathia gave their cabins, clothing, and food items to Titanic survivors, and did everything they could to aid. At 8:50 the Carpathia was home to 705 survivors of the Titanic and was headed to New York, though it was originally headed for the Mediterranean. Of of course it was the Carpathia wasn't the Titanic and was a far less elegant vessel hosted more people from the poorer classes. This meant that a lot of survivors were confined to the dining room and food was spread thinly between them. However, the warm reception of those aboard the Carpathia helped keep survivors alive.

In later discussions, how the ship sank Titanic challenged the statistical figures of survivors, saying that it was inadvisable to save children and women instead of the men or significantly more first-class passengers saved than those in third or second class the debate is still unresolved. Although men are an integral component of society, many think that it wasn't just the most honorable decision they could have made however, it was also crucial that women be saved alongside the children as they will be the next generation of the society. In addition, the statistics show that a fairly fair percentage of every class was saved, while the lower amount of passengers from third class is due to a range of circumstances that could not be addressed. First, a lot of them were in the deeper areas of the ship, which made it more difficult to reach the lifeboats. Secondly there were a lot of third-class passengers were not fluent in English and were unable to comprehend the need to get off the ship. However it turned out many have applauded those who were British for their equality of all the passengers as they believed that they were exemplary in the face of an extremely difficult circumstance.

While many lives were lost in the evening that the Titanic was sunk into a frigid and unforgiving sea There were a few that made headlines. The designer of the ship, Thomas Andrews, drowned as did a number of other members on the ship's crew, who gave themselves to save their passengers. Col. J.J. Astor, the richest man on the Titanic and among the most wealthy men of the world at the time - he was worth around 20 million pounds -- also was drowned. In the end Major Archibald W. Butt, an army veteran who served as an advisor for U.S. President Taft, was also killed.

Chapter 6: The Aftermath Of Sinking

"Titanic began a journey through time when it set sail away. A century later, there's still no port in sight." Marina Tavares Dias Marina Tavares Dias

In the aftermath of the tragic conclusion of the first voyage of the RMS Titanic, a public outrage and anger was apparent. The families who were victims of this tragedy seemed left in tears. In the end, the magnitude that the Titanic had sunk Titanic was put on the back burner however, the fury lasted for a long time.

It was hard to believe that this incident caused the deaths of more than 1500 people within the span of three hours was hard to accept. It was like a war that saw a town sunk to its demise and was drowned by the ocean's waters. Journalists employed charts, as well as other visual aids like photographs to determine the total number of victims which could be displayed to the general public. However, the process of determining the casualty lists was a major challenge in the aftermath of the maritime catastrophe.

The intensity of sea travel was thought to be safe, however the report of the sinking of Titanic RMS Titanic raised questions from the viewpoint of public, journalists, and government officials. The tragedy triggered an outcry that led to a formal investigation regarding the loss of life, one British and one American. In the course of time it was evident that the Americans were able to get by since the incident was studied by a variety of lawyers and academics.

British investigation was not thorough in its report on how the incident affected passengers and crew in the event that the vessel sinks because it did not have the authority to conduct a comprehensive investigation into the incident, and the procedure used in the American team was more focused and focused on the smallest aspects of the tragic incident. The procedure used in the British team was superior, however, the outcomes obtained through the American team offered a more accurate image of the entire incident. I'd like to share a passage from the report in The Los Angeles Times, dated April 19th, 1912 "Horror of the tragedy loom(ed) bigger with each passing hour". Each day the shadow of the sinking ship became more threatening. The number of deaths was becoming more precise. The scale of the tragedy was beginning to be felt.

The sinking RMS Titanic dates back to more than 100 years back. The incident led to a number of controversy and speculations about the incident. There are still speculations today in relation to the real reason for the tragedy and the kind of materials of steel used in the construction of the ship; scams relating to sabotage and insurance the music played when the sinking of the ocean liner; the trials of the captain Lord who was the captain of the Californian which did not respond to SOS messages from the RMS Titanic. The story of the liner and the myths associated with it continue to intrigue the human mind.

The tales of Titanic that have been passed on to the younger generations. Titanic which have now been passed on to the younger generation have been woven into every aspect of the tragedy that involved Titanic. RMS Titanic.

The incredible power that is Mother Nature to defeat humanity places greater importance on the location in which Titanic was sunk. RMS Titanic lies on the North Atlantic Ocean; it is more than just a site with archaeological significance However, the whole incident is a stark reminder of the gulf between prudential advancement and the rightful place for the dead.

The contemporary era has also served as a major source of controversy that has been relating to the collection of artifacts that were discovered from the wreckage. The tale of the sinking RMS Titanic continues to amaze everyone even in the present day. Many are still curious to learn more about what actually transpired.

Southampton, the city that was Southampton which was the boarding spot in the sinking of RMS Titanic, was experiencing the midst of a massive grief The family and close friends members were waiting anxiously at United States to welcome the passengers. Then media disruptions ruined people's excitement when they reported about the survivors who boarding the Carpathia the rescue vessel which was heading toward New York. Each newspaper from the majority of nations had published the names of those that survived, as well as those who died in the waters of the ocean. The first-hand data was collected by the reporters from details provided by the Mackay-Bennett an operator of cable steamers. The list of individuals that were identified as deceased was immediately distributed to media so that the nearest and close relatives of the deceased could receive the information regarding their loved ones in the shortest time possible. In particular, the public believed that the bodies of John Jacob Astor and Isidor Straus was buried away from the ocean's surface until the bodies of the deceased were recovered from the ocean The people were making improbable plans to recover the bodies that were submerged beneath the sea's surface.

The condolences started pouring through from every corner and nook across the world. But the families and survivors of the victims as one would expect, were devastated. The monarchs of England as well as the King George V and Queen Mary and Queen Mary, sent condolence messages to whole crew who work for White Star Lines for the loss caused by the tragic event. The royal family followed suit. condolence messages were sent out from Germany, Spain, Russia, France, Netherlands, and Belgium in protest of the tragic event.

The Procedure of Evacuation

The evacuation process started about an hour later or even more when it was discovered that RMS Titanic collided with an Iceberg in Newfoundland. The process of rescue was a mess and chaotic in the beginning when the initial group of passengers were transferred to the lifeboat. The most unfortunate thing was that the lifeboat was capable of carrying 65 passengers, but because of the poor education of its crew members in the field of safety , only 28 people were transferred to the lifeboat that was first manned. In the chaos that ensued prior to that the RMS Titanic finally sank into the bottom of the ocean as all lifeboats had fewer passengers than their maximum capacity. However, the lifeboats were able to save only a few passengers.

The maritime safety rules of the time of the disaster required evacuation of women and children first. The men were permitted to enter the lifeboat once the children and women were safely rescued. But the maritime safety regulations weren't properly followed because of the lack of knowledge of the of the ship's crew . As consequently, several women and children were also among people who were killed in deadliest shipwreck. But,

RMS Titanic belied the designer's hopes by staying steady and floating for a period of about three hours. The tragic loss revealed a variety of occasions of courage and also moments of low self-confidence and cowardice.

There's a lot of a slip between the lip and the cup and a number of dramas took place during the transfer of passengers into lifeboats for rescue and the last plunge in Titanic. RMS Titanic: chaos and chaos caused men to drift far from their spouses and as children. Families split apart, and humane people joined with their loved relatives or left their homes to aid a vulnerable passenger get away.

A distinguished crew faced the tragedy with calm and collected manner. They weren't a participant in the chaos or an anxious atmosphere. As an example, John Ismay provided his assistance in the process of evacuation. He helped a handful of passengers on the lifeboat, but could not get onto the lifeboat, and was unable to get aboard the ship. Even though there weren't any women or children on the vessel, he could be unable to live peacefully should he have been stranded alongside the drowning of others in the vicinity.

The architect who was the chief designer for RMS Titanic, Thomas Andrews was in the smoking area in First Class. First Class where he was immersed in a gorgeous artwork depicting one of the ships constructed in the late 1890s by White Star Lines. Astor assisted the pregnant Madeleine in the lifeboat first and asked her permission to assistance; her refusal led to him kiss her goodbye by kissing her goodbye. that the ship began sinking.

The perfect example of true love in this tragic event was the Isidor Straus and his wife Ida. The Straus couple decided to show their love for each other and, despite sitting and a table, the couple walked toward their cabin, where they would die together. Benjamin Guggenheim along with his valet went to his bedroom; dressed in formal evening dress, when they returned back to their deck saying "We are dressed to the nines in the best attire and ready to die like gentlemen".

Molly Brown was amongst the last passengers to get off the ocean liner while she assisted other passengers board the lifeboats. Instead of taking care of herself, she advised the the crew to help the passengers however they were scared by the idea of getting swept away in frozen ocean in an attempt to save the people who were crying out for urgent help. This is why Molly Brown is remembered for her selfless act to save passengers aboard Titanic's drowning RMS Titanic.

Operation of rescue conducted by the Carpathia

The RMS Titanic sank beneath the frozen seawater; the ship was sunk in a perpendicular inclination with all the lights glowing brightly. the clock was ticking beyond 2.20 a.m. The calendar showed April 15 1912. The Carpathia was among the vessels that played a vital role in helping save 705 people who survived the tragedy of. The ship was close to RMS Titanic and came to its aid in the midst of the time. RMS Titanic's crew broadcast SOS messages around midnight as the Carpathia came close to the ocean liner in full speed, getting past the icy dangers on the sea. The ship helped passengers who were aboard, those who were transported through lifeboats.

In addition to the technical failures that occurred during the disaster and the loss of RMS Titanic has left deeper wounds for future generations. The experts believe that we are not immune to the dangers of human foolishness. The laws of nature was stronger and nature displayed its strength, which made the "unsinkable" Titanic appear to be a minor task. Insanity ruined the fate of RMS Titanic as the ocean liner was sunk on the first voyage itself.

The incident also revealed the lack of knowledge on the part of the ships in the vicinity and the over-confidence of the designers and the inefficiency of the crew who were in charge of the ship. Initially it was reported that the ship's collision with an iceberg was described; however, the ship was able to remain afloat for three hours prior to being destroyed. The public was shocked to learn that even the most advanced technology was fatal.

Rumors began to circulate about the catastrophe that took place on RMS Titanic since the afternoon of April 15th 1912. Offices of shipbuilding company White Star Lines located in England and New York were ransacked by relatives, family members and acquaintances of passengers who were onboard to obtain information and update information about the evacuation procedure.

Chapter 7: The Survivors Of The Disaster

In the average of 2344 passengers on board the famous liner RMS Titanic to experience its debut voyage also an opportunity to experience a new stage of life. The Olympic-class ship was traveling from Southampton, England to the beautiful New York city. New York. Then, in the middle of their journey the ocean liner frozen iceberg sank the magnificent ocean liner on the 15th of April 1912. What followed was even more tragic as over 1500 persons were killed in the tragic accident.

As we've discussed in our previous chapter, passengers on the ship were divided into three different classes. Each class was determined by the social class and amount of money the passengers had. The most wealthy passengers travelled with the upper class. this included businessmen, top-ranking political figures, military personnel and athletes, etc.

Middle class passengers were with the class of second, they included authors and clergy members as well as tourists and professors. The passengers with the class of third sometimes referred to as 'steerage comprised immigrants looking to experience an entirely new way of existence in United States.

British Royal Family and Elites on RMS Titanic

It was also the day that members of the British Royal Family attended the occasion: The wife the XIX Earl of Rothes the Countess of Rothes arrived on board the ship at Southampton together with her parents as well as a her cousin. Another illustrious royal member on board the ship was Sir Cosmo Duff-Gordon V Baronet, of Halkin and Lady Duff-Gordon. A financier of the property's real estate sector was also aboard the ocean liner, with his name was Col. Archibald Gracie IV and he was a member from the Gracie family who was an American and Scottish and an American family. Lord Pirrie Chairman of Harland &

Wolff wished to embark on the first journey of RMS Titanic however, an illness kept him from the tragic event. It was the Cavendish of London is one of the most wealthy British couple was also on board. They were also joined by the MD as well as the designer for RMS Titanic, James Bruce Ismay and Thomas Andrews were present on the ship to observe how she was progressing on her debut voyage.

A Swedish businessman, Mauritz Hakan Bjornstrom-Steffansson, claimed the ownership of a French masterpiece i.e. an neoclassical painting with the title of La Circassienne at Bain.

American Elite Passengers onboard

American social elites didn't miss the chance to embark on the inaugural journey of RMS Titanic: Colonel John Jacob Astor IV and his wife Madeleine who were heading home to US to have their baby. Jacob Astor, a multimillionaire real estate property developer and businessman is believed to be the richest multimillionaire in the United States. Industry leaders

Benjamin Guggenheim, Isidor Straus and wife Ida, George Dunton Widener, George Dennick Wick, Charles Hays, William Ernest Carter, John Thayer, Lucile Carter, Margaret Brown, Karl Behr, Dorothy Gibson, Edward Austin Kent, and Major Archibald Butt were also travelling on the Titanic.

Do you think that the clergy members would have squandered this wonderful chance to travel in the Titanic? Not at all. Two RC priests Father Joseph Peruschitz and Father Thomas Byles were also on the ship. They were the ones who conducted every day Mass for passengers in the second and Third class aboard the ship. The homilies were offered in various languages such as German, English, Hungarian, French and the Irish.

The revered Baptist Pastor, John Harper, hailed from Scotland and sailed on the RMS Titanic along with his daughter and niece to bless the congregation of Moody Church located in Chicago.

A teacher in the field of Science, Lawrence Beesley, who taught at the Dulwich College was present on the ship the majority of the time as he was reading in the library for the first class. He was among the fortunate people who survived the devastating loss to the liner's ocean. A few years later, he wrote an account from the firsthand of the tragedy in his book "The Lost of the RMS Titanic'.

The Laroches family were also on the vessel; they comprised Joseph the father along with his twin daughters Louise and Simonne The Laroches were the only family members of black ancestry who was onboard the RMS Titanic. Joseph's wife Juliette was expecting; the family was planning to move from Paris to the Haiti island, which was their home homeland, to escape the racism.

Another French family traveling in the Second class were the Navratils name was a pseudonym for Hoffman. The family's head was named Michael Navratil was a French tailor originally from Slovakia He had abandoned his wife and fled with two sons. they were travelling under the fake identity as Louis M Hoffman. He had stepped aboard the ocean liner with the intent to remove his children from the eyes of their mother and head into the US.

Unfortunately the father died in the tragedy , leaving his sons in a state of despair. The information regarding the missing children was widely circulated to find their mother. The final outcome was that she came to France and claimed title of her children. The children were protected since they were looked after by the lovely Margaret Hays, until their mother arrived in New York.

The survivors of the TRAGEDY

The tragic loss of life that occurred during that ship's sinking Titanic resulted in the deaths of many passengers, however it is difficult how many the casualties and victims of the tragedy. A variety of reasons contribute to the uncertainty. One of them is a mismatch on passengers' lists since it contained names of passengers with cancelled travel plans. Additionally, a few passengers were travelling under false names and which led to double-counting. Analyzing the information revealed that the death count was at 1635 people.

A mere 1/3 of passengers on board the RMS Titanic were able to endure the tragedy. A few of those who survived the horrific accident died later and the cold sea water was painful and survivors also were unable to stand up to the cold and as a result of an enormous change in temperature they died after a short period of time.

The documents provide statistics on survivors, such as three female passengers in the first class were missing 54% of women on the 3rd class passed away children with the Ocean Liner's 2nd class survived, every one of them, and 52 children in the third class were killed.

A survivor alive at the time in the tragic event is Millvina Dean. In the tragic incident, Millvina Dean was only 9 weeks; he died in the month of May 2009, with a

97-year old age.. Violet Jessop, another survivor as well as a crew member was an important witness to the tragic sinking of RMS Titanic as well as the ship named Britannic as well as traveling on the Olympic at the time that the ship met with a minor collision in the year 1911.

Lifeboat 7 , the most important lifeboat launched on the Titanic's port that helped to evacuate 28 passengers who were much less than to the capacities of the Lifeboat i.e. 65 people. British inquiry says the Lifeboat 7 started its journey few minutes after midnight hour to help people escape the sinking vessel. Then, just two days later the last collapsible was launched to rescue the passengers. Lifeboats that were collapsibles weren't launched correctly due to the inefficiency of the personnel working on the vessel.

We've heard of stories that survivors were reluctant to get aboard the lifeboat because they were afraid that they would be swept off by sea water. Hence they tried to make it down the suction pipe on the liner. At around at 2:20 a.m. the liner sank into the ocean. Only a handful of passengers, along with crew members were able to free themselves from the lifeboats. They remained alive for a few hours after which they received the required assistance by Harold Lowe, the Fifth officer.

The clock hit 4:10 a.m. RMS Carpathia reached the scene of the tragic incident of the sinking Titanic. The ship began its rescue mission to transport survivors to shore. The clock now showed the hour as 8:30 am. the rescue vessel retrieved the last lifeboat for survivors and set off in the 8th minute at 8:30 a.m. It was reported that the RMS Carpathia was heading towards moving people who were rescued into Pier 54 located in New York. However, some survivors died in the entire journey.

Within a few days of the demise of the victims, recovery operations were conducted in the area. The ship-building business, White Star Line arranged for the chartering of chartered vessels to retrieve the bodies of dead victims. The ships that were sent to rescue operations comprised cable ship Minia as well as sealing ship Algerine as well as the lighthouse's supply vessel Montmagny. The company's rescue operations have recovered supplies, undertakers as well as the remains of a few clergymen. The bodies recovered were assigned a digit that gave a detailed account of the corpse to facilitate identification of the deceased. Other details like age, weight of the body, size and hair color, as well as the eye color tattoos, birthmarks, injuries, etc. were documented to notify their families accordingly.

The resources of counting the bodies and keeping the bodies were not sufficient due to the huge list of victims of the tragedy. A captain from the rescue vessel came to a decision to keep the bodies of the people who were traveling on the liner's first class because they believed in the strength of wealth and power. Therefore, many passengers with the class of third were omitted and forced to surrender their lives, and their bodies were dumped into the sea. Body parts that had been preserved were wrapped in plastic sheets and transported to the nearest city to be moved by steamships or railways.

Morgues were set up temporarily which relatives could take possession of their relatives' bodies. Assistance was offered by the morgue services in Eastern Canada as well. Families filled the morgues and came from all regions of Europe and North America. 150 bodies of the victims weren't claimed as the result, their bodies were put at the cemetery of their local.

I'd like to provide some details about two people who survived the tragedy of death.

The survivor who was attracted by the sight of the sinking vessel can be identified as Elizabeth Shutes; she worked as an governess. While she was on the RMS Titanic, she was just 40 years old. She assisted passengers as they moved toward to the Sun Deck once the ocean liner came into contact with the Iceberg. She remembers, "Our men knew nothing about the location of the stars, and they knew hardly what to do to pull them together. Two oars soon went in the water. The men's hands were just too frigid to hang on...Then in the water came that horrible scream that sounded like the cries of people who were drowning. To my ears, I heard"She's gone you guys, get rowing or we'll be the worst of the surge."

Another survivor that is traumatized by the nightmares of that dark night was Lawrence Beesley, a widower who is also a science teacher in London He was young when he took the RMS Titanic with a hope to see his brother, who was in Toronto. Beesley has written down his feelings and the horrifying images in his bestselling memoir , "The loss of the S.S. Titanic." The memoirs of his recommended strict recommendations to the government in order to avoid such types of maritime disasters. He also mentioned some of the myths that were disproved in the initial journey of RMS Titanic:"I will never repeat that 13 is a lucky number. Boat 13 is the most wonderful friend we've have ever met."

The tragic sinking and sinking Titanic is a compelling story for today's youth since it is the classic account of how recklessness and ignorance led to the deaths of many people. The scars from the tragedy are still in the hearts of descendants of survivors who are still eager to know about the true cause of the tragedy on the sea.

Chapter 8: Preparations For The "Monster" Type Of Ships

"I cannot think of any situation that could cause a vessel to sink. I can't imagine any major catastrophe happening for this boat. Modern shipbuilding has moved over the limits of."

Captain Smith of the Titanic. Titanic

The 1800s were just shifting into the 1900s, when enormous ocean liners became become hugely sought-after. These massive ships were designed to transport passengers (willing willing to shell out a premium price for tickets) to the other side of the world in complete fashion and with luxury. Around 1910, the most modern versions of the ocean liners were in operation. One of the major points of their development was the "Belfast shipyards" in Britain.

The shipyards were a source that was constantly energized and mobilized. A witness to the massive project was quoted as saying "For months and months within the enormous iron enclosure, there was nothing with any resemblance to a ship. There was only one thing that could be the iron scaffolding used for the naves of half a dozen cathedrals that were laid out from between the ends."

The story continues to say "At the end of the day, the skeleton inside the scaffolding started to take shape, and at the sight of which people were breathless. It had the form of the shape of a ship, one so massive and unbelievable that it loomed over the structures and was dwarfed mountains that were surrounded by water. A rudder as big as a giant elm tree, bosses and bearings of propellers the size of windmills--everything was on a nightmare scale; and underneath the iron foundations of the cathedral floor men were laying, on concrete beds, pavements of oak and great cradles of timber and iron and sliding ways of pitch pine to support the bulk of the monster when she was moved, every square inch of the pavement surface bearing a weight of more than two tons."

The ship was truly an enormous beast. As the story goes, "Twenty tons of tallow were spread over the pathways and hydraulic rams and triggers were constructed and fixed against the main body of the ship to ensure that when the moment arrived the seas they were to conquer would take her away from into the Earth."

The Titanic was certainly a stunning spectacle. It was built at the peak of steamship technology. It was designed to symbolise the triumph of mankind over the dark deep. While human beings had been navigating the seas for centuries, prior to the invention of the steam engine, human vessel was mostly dependent on nature's forces.

It was the winds in the sails on ocean-going vessels which kept them in the air. Steam ships could, however, sail against the wind if needed to. If coal was burning the steamship's engine could continue to propel the ship across the ocean. In a sense the Titanic became a symbol for the man's power over nature. In addition, the size of the ship was a way to emphasize the perceived power of man over the oceans.

As if the builder were attempting to make the ship sink, they constructed it as massively as they could. In the early 1910s the building of the Titanic was regarded as a major feat of engineering technology. The Titanic not only displayed the power of steam engines and a massive use of steel on wood. The use of steel was believed to have created a ship that was invulnerable to the harshness of the ocean.

Steel, naturally is certainly more durable than wood, but steel ships aren't invincible. It could be that it that over-confidence in the strength of steel that eventually caused a certain amount of carelessness in the operation of this brand new type of ocean liner. Since the introduction of steam-driven ocean liner, the cross-ocean shipping had become more durable and routine. It was within this environment that the shipbuilders from Belfast who built the Titanic--Harland and Wolff--came into the scene.

Harland and Wolff were a well-established company and operated their business on a "cost + model." This means that the business was able to build craft following specific, internal schematics, and once the project was completed there was there was a "fixed percent" could be added on the price. Under these circumstances when Harland and Wolff began to join forces with another group of ship experts situated at Liverpool, England, the known as the Ismay (after J. Bruce Ismay) and the Imrie Company, otherwise known as the "White Star Line."

The White Star Line came to prominence as a passenger and shipping ship business during the height of the British Empire, when Britannia reigned over the oceans. It was the White Star Line in the early 20th century served as an essential link in travel and commerce across the Atlantic and between Britain and the United States and Britain. White Star was responsible for numerous of the innovations in shipping that became popular in the latter half of the 1800s and the in the early 1900s.

White Star was considered top of the best when it came to transporting passengers. They took what was previously a long and tiring journey over the Atlantic and transformed into an industry that was centered around relaxation and comfort. In the same way that White Star had become experts in passenger transportation over the oceans, so shipbuilders Harland and Wolff were among the most skilled when it came to the construction of the ocean-going vessels.

Harland and Wolff were considered to be top of the line and were paid a lot of money to be able to perform their work. Also, they paid employees working in their shipyards at a more expensive rate than their peers in the time. They were also given an unspecified amount of money to build the most magnificent, grandest vessel of all time. Some critics criticized the efforts by referring to ships like that of the Titanic as "monster vessels." It was observed that these luxury ships were packing a lot of treasure and wealth inside their hulls, thanks to the expensive equipment. If one were to sink, it would cause an immense financial loss (not to not mention the loss of life).

The size of the Titanic class vessels also created problems, as the typical ports and harbors did not have the capacity to handle the massive size of these vessels. Changes must be developed in order to support the ship, and American taxpayers aren't pleased to pay the cost for the building of docks for the east coast of America. This issue was beautifully described in the latest issue of Engineering News.

The piece in question read in part "If the latest ocean monsters were a genuine breakthrough in transportation efficiency--

if their design resulted in lower costs for transatlantic freight transport, it is likely to be simple to answer both questions with a yes. There is there is no reason to think that these enormous vessels actually represent any kind of advancement. They were designed to offer the ultimate in luxury passenger travel. While they may represent an advancement in transportation efficiency the vessels could be the actual cost increase. It is interesting that the IMM White Star] and the IMM White Star] should undertake the construction of these massive vessels, without knowing in advance which port they would dock when they are finished with their journey. Given that the two companies have put themselves in a predicament and are in a bind, it might be the best option to let them figure out their own solution."

But, at the final, New York port officials gave in to pressure and utilized resources from the city to expand their docks in a way that could accommodate this massive class of ship. The modifications were then made and an object similar in size to the Titanic was named the "Olympic" arrived at New York harbor for the first time in 1911 and immediately following the heels of this giant came the Titanic. The Titanic amazed all who saw her. The exterior of the vessel was breathtaking, and everyone who visited the deck was amazed by the extravagant facilities that were on display inside.

It was because of the incredible coal-powered motor of the ship that the ship was equipped with the latest electrical technology. The engine that was powered by coal in the craft was able to power electronic devices of all kinds. The ship was equipped with refrigerators with electric elevators fitness equipment, an entire kitchen stocked with electric slicers and peelers, as well as various different food preparation tools. It was said to have used approximately 700 tons of coal every day and every single day, to power these elements of the craft.

Additionally powered by electricity were the hull doors that, with the flick of a switch could open to block off different parts of the ship in the event that they were weak. This was a crucial security feature that was installed on the vessel and it was believed that in the event of an accident the feature could suffice to prevent catastrophe.

With all this extravagant and luxurious, some even began to joke about the vessel as "the Millionaire's Special."The craft also featured clear distinctions between classes, thanks to making use of second, first and third-class categorizing of passengers. The most disadvantaged passengers on the vessel would be placed in the third class section, which had the passengers secured behind locked gates that prevented any mixing between the first- and second-class areas.

This may sound a little out of the realm of modern day perceptions, but the creators of the ship were determined to maintain a clear difference between people who paid a hefty sum of money to travel in first class and the ones who didn't. After its first voyage across the globe it was Titanic was returned to Britain arriving in Southampton Harbor on April 3rd 1912.

Then, on April 10, the newly tested ship was ready to embark on its first voyage with passengers who paid. From the passengers, it's estimated that 46% were first class passengers. People who booked first class were usually linked to wealthy industrialists. Some of them included Dick as well as Helen Bishop from the U.S. state of Michigan. The two Michiganders have become wealthy due to their stakes of the "Round Oak Stove Company."

They were newlyweds and had recently enjoyed a honeymoon trip to Europe and then purchased an all-first class ticket to board the Titanic for its epic voyage through the Atlantic to New York. Once in New York, they would travel back to Michigan to find a brand-new home was being constructed for the couple. For the young couple it was an incredible adventure, and the world was theirs. There was no way that anything could be wrong. They didn't realize the horrible disaster that would be waiting for them.

While many of the people associated with the Titanic have been described as arrogant snobs who believed that the ship was invulnerable to all dangers but there were a few prudent and cool heads behind these developments that were looking to add additional security features to this massive new passenger vessel. When the ship's handlers in Southampton swiftly checked the boxes on their list as the Titanic was ready to depart.

Titanic Sets Sail Titanic Sets Sail

"There is no risk that the Titanic sinks. The Titanic is unsinkable, and no inconvenience is likely to be incurred by passengers."

Phillip Franklin vice president of White Star Line

Following a great deal of fanfare, which included thousands of people gathering to watch the vessel sail away it, the Titanic began its voyage in the 10th of April in the afternoon 1912. The ship was led away from the harbor by its captain, Edward J. Smith. It was all going smoothly and yet, in the early stages the Titanic was in danger of crashing. Just after leaving the enormous suction generated after the Titanic when it steamed off the port produced an enormous backlash to the point that a nearby cargo ship--the New York -- was sucked straight out from the harbor, and almost being thrown into a collision in the direction of the Titanic.

It was only the keenness of Titanic's crew who was able to stop an accident from happening. The crew adjusted the engines of the ship and were able to reverse suction in a way to let another freighter ride through the waves towards the reverse far away from Titanic. With a collective sigh of relief the crew of the Titanic was able to escape into the open ocean unharmed. However, the Titanic did not immediately sail towards the west side of the Atlantic but instead turned around and visited harbors in the two countries of France and Ireland to take in, and even more payed customers.

It was at this point that the ship began its journey towards America's northern shores. Based on the reports of survivors' eyewitnesses on the initial leg of the journey, passengers who were aboard had an enjoyable time. They were playing tennis in the large gymnasium, eating lavish meals and, according to reports, taking part in the most popular activity of all--riding in and out of elevators.

Elevators were a bit of an innovation in 1912, therefore, the possibility of having one on an ocean vessel was more thrilling. The excitement would diminish only a few days later with the announcement that the Titanic hit an Iceberg. The risk of renegade floating glaciers in the northern parts of the Atlantic was at a higher danger at the time due to the relative warm temperatures of the winter before.

The warmer temperatures caused huge chunks of ice to split from Greenland and drift to the south to the sea lanes that comprise North Atlantic. That meant huge chunks of ice were waiting in the middle to one of the most traveled routes of the sea between Britain as well as North America. There had been a number of close encounters with other ships in actual fact, including the nearly fatal encounter between an iceberg with a ship named the Niagara.

The ship was taking the exact same journey over into the North Atlantic that the Titanic was expected to make, but it was also struck by an Iceberg. Fortunately for Niagara, even though the bottom of the ship was damaged by ice, the vessel managed to make it to a safe harbor in New York before completely filling with water. The Titanic was not as fortunate.

As terrifying as the Titanic catastrophe could seem, as previously mentioned story of the Niagara clearly demonstrates the fact that icebergs posed a floating danger within the North Atlantic was common knowledge. Also, the Titanic was informed prior to the time the radio operator of another vessel, the Californian, sent an alert to the Titanic radio operator Jack Philips.

Philips was having a great experience with the Titanic's latest Radio system that was in constant trouble throughout the time. While quietly looking over the radio system, he was stunned when his switchboard was activated, and there was an alarming voice that warned of an ice. Jack Philips was startled and annoyed. He was so angry, in fact, for him to shout out at Radio operator "Shut up! Shut up! I am busy."

In the past, it's easy to critique the insanity and possibly naivete the Radioman Jack Philips, but he certainly couldn't have foreseen the catastrophe the Titanic was set to experience. In any case, it was shortly before midnight hour, when the ship sailed across into the North Atlantic, that crewman Frederick Fleet, from his position within the "crow's nest" of the vessel, noticed an iceberg soaring right within the path of Titanic.

He. Fleet raised the alarm with an alarm. A bridge officer asked the captain, "What do you see?" And fleet answered, "Iceberg!" The crew then reacted and turned the ship to the left in an effort to escape the floating ice mass. They avoided collisions head-on, however the saying goes that this was just the top of the iceberg. although they avoided the huge mass of ice, they could still observe above the water The larger structure of ice below the watersurface, smashed against the lower hull the Titanic when it passed.

In doing so the ice, which was rock hard, managed to cut a hole in the steel structure of this ship. For the majority of people aboard the vessel it was an unimportant incident. The incident wasn't even thought of as an incident. Many were asleep and were asleep for the entire time. However, not all. One woman who lived to see the Titanic's sinking--Sylvia

Caldwell--remembers having woken up to a feeling of shaking of the ship. The sensation she described was like "a large dog that had the baby kitten inside its mouth, and it the ship was shaking."

A majority of passengers were unaware of the accident, and when they did, they quickly forgotten about it and went onto other matters. However, significant damage was caused to the outer hull of the Titanic and shortly thereafter, the gash would appear on its right side, and the lower part of the Titanic started to seep water. It was only an issue of time before the entire craft went under. Many of the crew didn't know -- or they didn't even realize the magnitude of the danger they were placed in.

In the deck above after the remnants of ice and snow made their way onto the bridgedeck, some were able to take part with each other in "snowball battles." This may have may have helped calm jitters and play in the snow however it didn't help solve the Titanic's troubles. By ten minutes before midnight, the entire portion of the front part of the lower decks was inundated with water and the ship was beginning to slide to the side.

Captain Smith while waiting for his ship looked at a particular instrument aboard called the "commutator" which can measure the extent to which a vessel is letting down, or leaning on its side. He was amazed to find that the vessel is "listing two degrees lower than the bow and five degrees towards the port." For people who aren't acquainted to sailing terms have no significance but the response of this experienced captain when he saw them, leads us into the severity and seriousness of what was happening. When he saw this readout, Smith gasped, "Oh My God!"

Then, he immediately went below deck to see the destruction directly. After seeing the flood at the lower deck, Smith very quickly came to the conclusion that the Titanic was on the verge of sinking to the bottom of the ocean , like the steel-hulled, heavy rock. Alongside the captain during the inspection was no other than the Harland Managing Director and Wolff, Thomas Andrews.

The designer of the ship should know the insides and outs of the Titanic more than any other and believed it was a fact the Titanic was in danger of being destroyed. Andrews was aware of the fact that Titanic was constructed with a variety of compartments that could be sealed; because of the massive damage the majority of them could not seal properly, and were swiftly becoming flooded. The captain was aware that the ship had to be evacuated. However, there was a small issue: there were not enough lifeboats on the ship to save all passengers.

Captain Smith believed he had an advantage by making use of the radio on board to call an additional craft nearby that might be able to assist in the evacuation. Smith issued a distress signal across to the nearby vessels but the closest craft to receive the call was a ship known as the "Carpathia" located fifty miles away. The ship was not successful in reaching them on time. Captain Smith was in a bind however he was forced to take action, and so the captain issued an order to passengers must take off their "life protecters."

The moment was later remembered by an Titanic survivor, Laura Mabel Francatelli. Laura was an employee to a famous heiress known as Lady Duff Gordon. Laura was working with Lady Duff along with the husband of her, Sir Cosmo when a crew member arrived at their front door and informed them that it was determined that the passengers must wear "life protectors" to show precaution.

While no explanation was provided however there was everyone in the ship that something was seriously wrong. Soon, a number of people wearing life jackets were pouring on the decks to try and learn more about what happened to the Titanic. The water levels below deck during the time was becoming more severe. Despite the valiant efforts of crew members to remove excess water, it proved to be an unsuccessful battle, which meant that the boat was at risk of sinking.

It was at 12:45 am when "distress rockets" began to roar to the sound of. They were incendiary firecrackers that were lit, released into the sky, just to be ready in the event that a traveling through the region could be able to spot the rockets. The lifeboats in the meantime began to be loaded up with passengers--primarily women and children--and set down, just outside of the Titanic's steel hull.

In a demonstration of the length of time it took the seriousness that was the situation become apparent among the people on board, the initial lifeboat was only able to accommodate 28 people boarding. Then, frenzied passengers were trying to get onto lifeboats. However, at this point, the passengers were not aware what risk they were in, and were waiting their turn. It was the Titanic was still filling up with water at one hour, and when it was one o'clock the next morning, the forward bow portion of the ship dropped its head under the waves.

At the end of the day, around 2500 people perished and make that the Titanic an event that is considered to be among the most devastating shipwrecks in the history of maritime transport. However, there were many survivors who lived to tell their horrific stories. The next section we'll provide their riveting descriptions of what it was like aboard the Titanic when it went down.

Chapter 9: Putting Together The Stories Of Survivors

"Many brave acts were performed during the night, but none was as brave as the few musicians who played for minutes on end as the ship slowly sank lower and lower into the ocean. The music was played as their own eternal funeral requiem, and they had the privilege of being immortalized in the rules of unending fame."

Lawrence Beesley Titanic survivor

People who survived the single most devastating maritime catastrophe in the history of mankind had a compelling story to relate. However, it could be difficult for historians to construct an overall narrative out of the many fragmented versions of the events. Sure, the blockbuster film "Titanic" featuring Leonardo DiCaprio and Kate Winslet was a great job of highlighting key elements, but understanding the true chronology could be a bit difficult.

Based on what we know that it was at around 12:45 when the lifeboats started to be loaded. One of the survivors--Dorothy Gibson--recollects being "jostled" by crowds of screaming people before being taken in one of lifeboats. She was then in the lifeboat along with her mother and others and the frigid wind violently whipping around their backs.

A soldier known as Thomas Sloper had helped Dorothy to get in the lifeboat and, afterward Dorothy refused to take his hand and demanded that he join them on the boat. This stance could have saved Thomas the day, because unlike most of his male counterparts Thomas listened to the call to board the lifeboat and avoided being sunk by the sinking vessel.

It was while the first lifeboats were being filled up that a particular Mrs. Beckwith recalled having a encounter with the shipping magnate Ismay. She asked Ismay if she thought there could be enough lifeboats available for all. To thisquestion, she will later remember, Ismay replied, "Of course, Madam. All passengers, males and women, travel on these vessels." Ismay should know that this was not an issue, however maybe the reason he was not keen to cause fear by acknowledging that some passengers might have to be abandoned.

A lot of men were already painfully aware of this fact because they were being kept from children and women and were preferred to be boarding lifeboats. A few of the men nevertheless, were willing to put aside chivalry, should they need to in order to save themselves. On one occasion, it's said that a certain Dr. Henry William Frauenthal and his somewhat rotund brother--Isaac--leaped into one of the lifeboats, without permission, just as it was being lowered.

The huge model of Isaac was unable to strike the lifeboat's deck with ease However, it ended up hitting ramrod ding directly into the female passenger, named Miss. Annie May Stengel. The man landed upon her with enough force that he broke her ribs and struck her in the face with the force of the hit. The angry passengers started screaming to get the man taken off the boat. Perhaps realizing just how insignificant the act could be (and likely to be difficult due to the weight of the man) they finally bowed and let the stowaway remain where they were.

Some men, however in the midst of the grief of loved ones didn't hesitate to stay at home. Titanic survivors Julia Cavendish would later recall her and husband Tyrell who was woken up from their sleep by the chaos of the deck above they were escorted to an emergency lifeboat. The boat was able to assist her on the boat however she was shocked to watch her husband disappear in the crowd. Tyrell had either realized it or was quickly informed that he was not allowed to board the vessel, but was not able to resist.

Another person who had an enduring memory of the last moments with loved ones -- at least two--was Helen Churchill

Candee. She was. Candee is described as 53 years old American "writer as well as divorcee." In those times, divorce was uncommon than it is now. Just because you were an "divorcee" you were instantly a unique individual.

In the way of attracting Candeee. Candee, was the fact that she was stunning to look at. While on the Titanic the ship, she was involved in a couple affair with two men. She was seen on the move with the London investor who was named Hugh Woolner as well as an New Yorker, named Edward Kent who was a highly successful engineer.

Before leaving the Titanic her mother had left Kent the gold flask bearing her name on the lid. In the end, his body was later discovered floating in the water, and the same gold flask in his possession. Even though the request to "ladies first" was issued, not all female passengers aboard the Titanic were excited to make the jump from the ship's side and into one the lifeboats floating in the water off the ship's side.

Edith Rosenbaum would later recall her own hesitation as well as how she had been forced to join lifeboats. It was just after one at dawn, and with the ship still being filled with water, and sinking further and more into the water when Ms. Rosenbaum ran into none other Bruce Ismay.

The Mr. Ismay, who appeared to be shocked to see her wandering around, is believed to have yelled "What is it that you're being doing aboard this vessel? I thought that all children and women were gone! If there are more children and women on the ship, they should take a step forward and get to the stairway right away."

Edith stated she was pushed by Ismay had then shoved her down a staircase to the deck. In the open deck two rough-and-tumble sea-farers handcuffed her, and she was half-dragged and half-shoved to the lifeboat as she exclaimed, "Don't push me!" The sailors, probably aware that they'd soon die and wish they could be on the lifeboat at Edith's request and show their displeasure by screaming, "If you don't want to leave, stay!"

The crew then let her go and then made the decision to allow her to drown due to not cooperating. Edith will later remember her experience that among the main reasons for why she was having a difficult time was her skirt was a skirt that was long, that would have made getting over the railing and getting into the lifeboat challenging. The male passenger Philip E. Mock close by, seemed to be able to comprehend her situation and offered his help.

He sat down and let Edith to rest her feet on his knee. As she placed her arm on his throat, so she could make use of his body as a platform to get over the railing and then drop in the lifeboat. It was a success and within a short time Edith was inside the lifeboat, along with others waiting to be released from the ship that was sinking.

As the situation became more dire, some men decided to defy the seemingly sworn rule of putting girls and women first, and attempt to jump onto the ship.

A man whose name is not known to us, but is described as the "Italian immigrant" got into a lifeboat only to be dragged back out. The man was then allegedly brutally beaten by an angry crowd on deck who mocked the man for his alleged "cowardice" in wanting to protect himself.

One survivor was an British man with his name Gus Cohen would later reveal his determination to make it through even though he had an escape attempt from Titanic blocked. Gus was just aged 18 in the year he was killed, was staying in the lowest section of the Titanic, a third class. Unfortunately, as a special treatment was given to first-class customers, this resulted in Gus less valuable than other passengers.

Gus recognized this for his own self, but was determined to beat the odds. Being aware that he'd be treated more favorably if people believed that he was from the first-class section Gus tried to sneak into"the "first Class deck." However, when he tried to enter the third class section, he was confronted by a group of big, muscular mariners, who shouted at him to go back to the third class.

Gus tried to comply with the request, however being aware that doing so would be basically the death penalty and he continued to poke around the floor of the ship and eventually managed to sneak to the first-class deck unnoticed by guards. However, to this day, being deemed a first-class male is not enough to get a seat in the lifeboat. Even among the first-class passengers seats were generally reserved for children and women--and in addition, many were at or near capacity. Gus like many others , would come up with a solution.

Mr. Ismay In the meantime, he stood firm with the ship's captains in an effort to maintain order and avoid unjustified stowaways. It wasn't until Ismay, along with his fellow deckhands, believed that all the children and women had gotten onto lifeboats that he started to think about his personal safety. Ismay stumbled across the "collapsible vessel" and climbed aboard it. Although it is claimed that Ismay may have put the needs of the other passengers above his own, the reality the ship did not sink with the ship would be a cause for suspicion from the public, as well as his own personal guilt of being a survivor could haunt his throughout the rest of his life.

One of the people who later criticized Ismay was another fellow Titanic survivor Jack Thayer. Thayer who was just 17 years old at the time, young at the time will later remember Ismay as somewhat agitated, when he tried to get onto the last ship. Thayer did not view Ismay's actions as heroic in all , but instead saw Ismay as being displaying simple and selfish self-sufficiency. Thayer was, on the other hand was aboard the Titanic nearly to the end of the line when he and his friend Milton Long contemplated what to do next.

They were aware they had to realize that any endeavor to climb onto one of the lifeboats that were left was a huge challenge and the only alternative was to just dive headfirst into the sea. Because the cold, icy water could shut off your heart, as well as hypothermia was also a probable possibility, even for those who were skilled swimmers and a good swimmer, a plunge into those cold water was not an appealing choice.

Jack was not sure whether his family was able to make it through However, his mother Marian actually had discovered an emergency lifeboat. It was when the Titanic abruptly sank towards a near vertical angle and appeared close to being completely submerged at any time it was at this point when Jack took his final crucial choice. He left his friend Long whom he just met on the journey but during the very few intense moments it was as if the two of them had been friends for a long time.

The two exchanged handshakes, before they both bailed the ship and jumped off the railing and plunged into the freezing water. The cold water had a rapid effect, freezing his body to the bone, creating oxygen in the back of his body. He was nearly suffocated but was able to get back control and swim back towards the water's surface. In a struggle to stay sane in the frigid waters as he looked around to observe the Titanic rapidly sinking to the depths of the sea.

The ship was almost completely vertical and only a tiny part of it was above the water. The highest point of the Titanic was perched on a precarious ledge as if it were only the tip of a artificial iceberg that was protruding from the depths. Surprisingly, the screaming passengers could be seen desperately hanging onto the railings on the upper deck. This was certainly a desperate decision, considering that the effort to hold onto the railing for as long as they could not stop them from sinking when the entire ship was submerged.

Thayer later remembered thinking that the passengers who were hapless looked like scared "swarming honeybees." Thayer and other survivors heard the huge blast of boilers blasting up, dislodging themselves from their shackles, before plunged into the deep. The same happened to the remaining passengers on the Titanic.

The the Rescue Ship and the Widow Ship

"To my fellow sufferers My heart is filled with sadness for you all and is filled with sadness that you're weighed down by this burdensome load that was imposed on us. We pray that God be with us and be with us everyone."

--Eleanor Smith is the widow of Titanic's Captain Smith

Edward J. Smith, captain of the Titanic.

Following the time that the Titanic was completely submerged into the ocean and a floating armada lifeboats and dinghies remained scattered across the frigid sea. The survivors could see a few specks of light emanating from the flashlights used by those trying to navigate the fragile craft. Although these survivors had made it through the sinking Titanic however, at the moment there was no assurance that they would survive to tell the story.

They were still trapped in the middle of freezing cold waters, and no one could be sure whether someone would ever arrive to help them. The good news was that the Carpathia was the vessel that received a distress call by the Titanic and was only several miles away from where they were. They crew members on the Carpathia were aware that it was crucial to be on time but they also knew they had to be aware of the possibility that they were to also be hit by an iceberg in the frigid waters, and then end with the same fate similar to the Titanic prior to them.

It was around 4 am when the Carpathia was within sight. Being aware that lifeboats would be in close proximity the captain of the vessel put numerous flares, in order to inform survivors that help was in the pipeline. Then, shortly after the Carpathia carried the first survivors from lifeboats. They were the ones from whom they discovered the shocking reality, that the Titanic was lost beneath the sea.

As the Carpathia faced Lifeboat upon lifeboat was becoming increasingly difficult to carry passengers aboard. Some were frozen stiff that they needed to be carried onto the boat using ropes and huge "coal bags." The dawn sun's rays could be seen above the horizon as lifeboats were loaded on the decks of Carpathia.

The sun was rising, and the icebergs that sat in the surrounding waters took on an impressive appearance. Like golden, glowing mountains, it was difficult to reconcile this considering that one of these incredible images had resulted in the death of many passengers aboard the fateful Titanic. When it was decided that there was no more survivors, the process of helping those who survived began. The frozen bodies were all frozen and required medical attention.

After the first steps were put in place to protect your body, it was the process of resolving their tense minds that will be their largest challenge. Captain of the Carpathia, Vaughn, would later say, "They were glad to be alive but overwhelmed with grief over the deaths of sons, fathers brothers, husbands and a myriad of dear friends." It is said that Vaughn himself was forced to work to hold himself together to ensure that he didn't get overwhelmed by the grief.

The harsh reality began to was settling in for all the women who lost husbands, fathers and sons, the grief was overwhelming. Many began to refer to the Carpathia being"The "Widow Ship" due to the large amount of widowed, grieving women that were on board the ship. This was indeed a sad situation, but this was a situation that the people who were in charge of the vessel were required to remove from their minds in order to live.

They were the ones who couldn't get the ache and fear out of their minds who suffered the most. One of the passengers on the Carpathia One Mathilda Weisz, later recall women being devastated by the loss of loved ones that they had no choice but to contemplate suicide. At least on once, the woman observed one woman who "was very depressed manner and was preparing to leap."

An Titanic survivors, Madeleine Mellenger, also spoke of the grief of the survivors. She recalled an individual by the name from Jane Laver Herman who was so stricken with grief, she would talk about her suicide before anyone was willing to listen. As Madeleine will later remember, "She was almost insane in the Carpathia I remember as I was in someone's cabin for the entire day, not knowing the location of my mother. Mrs. Herman threatened to commit suicide, and for me, as a young person, it was an unforgettable experience. I was crying all day long."

The widows who travelled to the Carpathia but ended up becoming despairing human beings. Some of them were able to endure and, despite the odds, even were able to find love. Like the recently widowed young lady named Eloise. It seems quite snooty to claim that the recently widowed woman had a relationship to a man who survived who was on the Carpathia and it's more or less what transpired.

Eloise will later remember the sequence of events that eventually led to her second marriage together with another lost soul who escaped the destruction from the Titanic. Like many other survivors tales, it all started with that fateful night on April 14th. She was out enjoying the outdoors with her newlywed wife, Lucian Phillip Smith, a 24-year-old woman whose family had grown wealthy from coal mining-- and chatting it about with her acquaintances before retiring to bed at around 10:30 pm.

It was just after midnight when Eloise was awakened by her husband with information that the vessel was hit by an

Iceberg. According to her later account her husband wasn't any way concerned about the incident. He even stated that the ship had suffered only minor damage. Lucian believed that the journey from New York would merely be delayed, if not delayed.

But, Lucian informed his wife that an order was made to put "all ladies present on deck." The idea of having to be dragged out of bed and put on the deck was alarming, however, Lucian continued to minimize the whole situation, saying that it was normal procedure. As he said as a simple "formality." Lucian either thought that everything was in order or was simply making an act of faux show for the sake to his spouse.

However, Eloise consented to the order, and after putting on "her heavy clothes with high heels, heavy clothing, along with two jackets" she took her husband Lucian on board of the vessel. In the end nevertheless, in spite of her husband's protests she did go back into her cabin to take a couple of precious rings that her husband purchased for her. Lucian appearing to act like the whole thing was a kind of drill, warned her for having such items completely unnecessary, but let her take them nonetheless.

After that, the couple walked hand in arm until they reached the point the area where passengers were taken to lifeboats. Because Lucian had just mentioned that he needed to be on deck but not about getting into a lifeboat Eloise was somewhat confused. Once she was asked to take a boat however, she was shocked to discover that her husband wasn't going to be with her. She demanded the captain nearby for permission to let her husband go but he refused to glance at her, but just kept calling"woman and children first! "woman as well as children" first!"

If it was a drill, it quickly turned into a frightening one. However, Lucien kept up the pretense that everything was in good hands. As she was about to break off from the man she was married to, her husband looked at her and said, "I never expected to have you obey me but this is an occasion when you have to; it's just an issue of formality to allow women and children first. The boat is well-equipped and all the passengers is safe."

With such statements of apparent conviction, it makes one wonder what was going on in Lucien's head. Was he really believing the words he spoke of? Perhaps he was just trying to keep his young wife from being scared? Whatever the reason however, when Eloise inquired whether he was telling the truth, he affirmed that the truth was his, before kissing goodbye to her. Then she was put in the lifeboat, and was able to watch when her husband turned away before disappearing into crowd of passengers in the decks of the Titanic.

Eloise along with her fellow lifeboat crew members were then dropped down into the frigid water below. Eloise did not know what was happening, but she was sure that her secure husband was aware on the current situation. Amazingly, after having observed the ship breaking into pieces and sink, despite the screaming of the remaining Titanic crew and passengers when they fell under, she was convinced that her husband had to be aboard a different vessel or had discovered a way to escape.

From the moment of her arrival on the rescue vessel Carpathia actually, Eloise figured her husband was alive. Only after speaking to other survivors, that she realized that this was definitely not the situation. One of the survivors she spoke with, was one of the Titanic survivor rare-- a young male. Robert Williams Daniel, the male survivor proved to be a huge comfort and played a crucial role in bringing Eloise into the realization that her husband of just a few months was dead.

Robert was introduced to her as a comforter. He greatly eased her grief, thanks to his own experiences as a survivor too and his job would later evolve from comforter to a new romantic partner. Eloise was married to Robert were married just two years following the sinking the Titanic in the summer of 1914. It's a heartwarming and romantic tale however, it is marred by the grim reality of Robert's own demise. We can now see the romantic ideas from the Titanic as somewhat absurd.

In the immediate following of the Titanic anyone who survived the Titanic was usually viewed with great suspicion. It was a question of how they be alive? In the context of when it was stated to be the case that "women or children" were the first to be considered and that men were disposable What was the way this man get into the lifeboat? Did he sneak onto the boat? All speculations about Robert's survival has led to charges of cowardice.

In the years, he would mention his personal story in a less frequent manner. Investigators later tried to inquire from family members about specifics about his escape from the Titanic and be disappointed with the outcome. A family legend suggests that the man jumped off and then was able to swim towards an iceberg hanging onto the edge of the ice until later picked up by a second lifeboat.

Many dismiss such a scenario as unlikely, but not impossible at all. Because Robert was smacked into silence many years ago, there was not much else to base the conclusion on. But, regardless of the circumstances of how Robert was able to survive, Eloise was grateful for his support and love. be a part of, regardless of how it happened.

Though he might not be crying out in public, another person who was unhappy with the incident was the then sitting U.S. president--William Howard Taft. The president Taft was observantly watching the events unfolding on the Titanic and not only as it happened to be a huge disaster and also because one of his advisors to the president--Major Archibald Howevert--was on the vessel.

President Taft determinedly hoped that his aide survived as did many survivors of the Titanic looking for his loved ones constantly made contact to determine whether Archibald survived from his position in DC. He also took the action. In the event of a disaster, Taft was able to scramble the two "scout cruisers" the "Salem" and the "Chester" to travel towards the spot of the sinking and check if they might be helpful.

The two ships were charged with coordinating with the Carpathia to receive a complete account of Titanic survivors. Unfortunately the President Taft was later to discover about the fact that Captain Archibald Butt went down with the ship. There were more urgent issues to consider with respect to survivors in the time since the majority were left with nothing after Titanic's sinking. Titanic.

Likely, a lot of those who survived were widows or orphans. It's important to remember that, in 1912, it was not common for women to be able to pursue her own job and, in turn, many were completely dependent on the earnings from their spouses. With a large number of widowed women and abandoned children, a pressing issue was posed on how to provide a suitable financial aid to the plight of all these poor survivors.

Through the "Red Red Cross Emergency Relief Committee" that $130,000 was raised for particular aid to "Titanic survivors." The chairman of the committee was Robert W. de Forest.

It was the late Mr. de Forest who put out a directive which reads, "Most of the payments must be handled as pensions and are placed under the ongoing supervision of responsible agencies. This kind of assistance is particularly important for widows' families. Seventy-two have already been identified to the committee, out of which sixty-three lost their husbands during the tragedy. A few have returned back to England or other regions of Europe and receive the bulk of the relief through the funds collected from abroad."

The Red Cross was required to ensure that they weren't getting swindled during the procedure. A Red Cross representative--W.

Frank Persons, discovered that not everything is as it appears. Mr. Persons was interviewing survivors and it was during a conversation with a young man his name, Burke who was a survivor, that he stumbled to what he believed was a horrific account of tragedy and survival. Burke is from England and was booked in a third class seat on the Titanic for a trip toward New York, in an attempt to begin a new life in America.

When he was in his teens, Burke claimed that he was an orphan prior to embarking on the Titanic and that he was traveling with their sister Alice Catherine Burke, along with him on his journey towards New York, so that they could both have an opportunity to start over. Burke claimed that he was an orphan. Burke claimed that he was able to sneak onto a lifeboat and another passenger , after hearing his story of heartbreak, helped conceal him by hiding him in her coat. When he was at the water, he was found and a few passengers started arguing at the thought of throwing the man into the sea however, eventually they gave in and the man was allowed to remain.

Burke says it was his sister who was fortunate, and she had died. Burke then was able to inform Mr. Persons that his sister was wearing a gold chain on her neck that contained her initials on it at the time that she went missing. Persons was moved by the story, but quickly realized that it was just a fabricated story. An orphan that claimed to be was 14 was in fact significantly older, possibly older than 20 years of age.

Then it was found out that his entire tale was concocted and there was nothing truthful in it. It was discovered that Mr. Burke was just a fool, using his deceit (if it was as a gift?) to swindle his way into the lifeboat. But by Thanksgiving 1912 it was the time that there was a Titanic Relief Fund had been created to provide charity aid to all the widows and orphans who are truly in need of help.

The fund was initially able to raise $62,010. The amount was then surpassed with that of the British aid fund that was able to raise 2 million dollars. This amount is considered to be assistance in times of need. In addition to the sheer amount of money an additional fascinating pieces of aid came from an Titanic survivor. Margarette Brown, who would later be referred to as"The Unsinkable" Molly Brown.

The late Ms. Brown had already been recognized for her bravery during when the ship sank. Titanic. From the beginning to the final moment Ms. Brown was seen helping others to get into lifeboats not concerned about her own safety. Only when crew members pressured her that she entered a lifeboat on her own.

Even so, she managed to persuade the captain of the boat to change direction to look for survivors. There are reports that say the captain initially refused and Molly or threatened to throw her or herself overboard until he accepted. After getting picked up by Carpathia Molly. Brown who was herself a wealthy woman, set up her own charitable foundation to assist the survivors.

The group was dubbed"Survivors Committee "Survivors Committee" The group was formed to gather resources to helping the Titanic survivors, who were the most vulnerable and in need. It was definitely admirable of her to act in this manner, as the most vulnerable survivors were often the ones that were least noticed.

In addition to assisting with the basic necessities of life In addition to providing basic welfare, Ms. Brown, demonstrating her awareness of the trauma that her passengers suffered she also made sure the committee secured counseling for psychiatric issues to those who needed it. A large number of Titanic survivors would certainly be grateful for the work of the unstoppable Molly Brown. It was hoped that each kinds of assistance could in the healing process of those who managed to survivor the sinking of the Titanic.

Chapter 10: The Survivors Go Home

"About the time that people started jumping off the stern. My friend Milton Long and myself stood next to each other and both leapt onto the rail. We didn't send each other messages to get return home as neither of us believed we'd return."

Jack B. Thayer, Titanic survivor

On the 18th of April 1912, people from New York, and really most of the world, had their attention focused on the harbor. It was because it was on that day that the Carpathia -a vessel packed with Titanic survivors was returned to dry ground. In addition to the interest from the public at large, the event was of particular curiosity to relatives who were yet to discover the location of their relatives.

In the months leading up to this return to home, what were known as "passenger checklists" of the survivors were repeatedly written and rewritten. Although these lists offered some idea of who might be alive however, there was always a possibility that someone could be missing. In the gloom of despair that relatives who hadn't seen the names of their relatives that were listed in the lists of survivors flooded the docks, with hope that their relatives were not missing, and were in good health.

The media was all out to cover this tragic event, hoping to gather fascinating personal interest stories of people who survived the tragedy and their concerned families. The reporters also wanted to find answers to the most challenging questions that surrounded the entire Titanic tragedy. They sought to inquire with officials about the reason the reason why this luxurious liner, which was said to be almost indestructible--sank like a rock to depths of the Atlantic.

Prior to the sinking of the Titanic the most significant maritime drama was when Admiral Dewey destroyed a complete Spanish armada of waters in 1898, and brought closure to the Spanish-American

War. In a way, the entire Spanish-American War was sparked with another maritime disaster, the sinking USS Maine. However, in the past the idea that Spain actually sank the Maine is in serious doubt.

It was in the early hours of April 18th that Brooklyn Naval Yard Brooklyn Naval Yard received a radio broadcast message. The message, which came from an scout boats that was dispatched by President Taft to read the names of each of the survivors of the third class. It is interesting to note that, even though the scout ship had made an official request from Taft to obtain information on his missing advisor to the president Archibald Butt, the Carpathia was not able to permit the information to be communicated.

For reporters in the area the incident proved to be an interesting headline as soon as newspapers were covered with headlines such as, "TAFT WIRE REFUSED BY RECURING the vessel." The newspaper's editorial staff was able to spend hours trying to determine why this might be the scenario. There was speculation the possibility of "censorship" in the making as well as speculation that maybe old Ismay could be trying to hide the truth from the eyes of everyone.

There was an uneasy feeling between the general public and those who were in charge of the Titanic and the fabricated tales only exacerbated the anger that was already felt. However, before the arrival of the Carpathia significant strides were taken to ensure that the survivors' return be as smooth as it could. To guarantee the complete security (not to be forgotten privacy) of passengers, huge fences were constructed in order to guard people who exited the Carpathia.

Additionally, NYPD was out in full force to ensure that the crowds of people watching and journalists remained away from the survivors who were rushing in. In consideration of the requirements of a lot of the passengers in third class Special arrangements for humanitarian assistance were made between immigrants community leaders who resided in New York. According to reports, there were "Hebrew, German, Irish, Italian, and Swedish Immigration Societies" of the time were all pooling their resources to offer accommodations to Titanic survivors who required it.

It was thought that the wealthy first-class passengers were well looked after by the estates of their families. So it was inevitable that the requirements of those in third class who were poor started to dominate. Organisations like The Red Cross and The Sisters of Charity were present and ready to shoulder the bulk of the relief burden. Even the head of New York Giants, John T. Brush--joined in the game, inviting his team to participate in an exclusive "exhibition game" to raise funds for the most disadvantaged in survivors of the Titanic survivors.

As the arrival of survivors drew near, people began gathering around Cunard pier at around 6 o'clock that night in hope of getting some glimpses of the action. Around 8pm the crowd were gathered, with each one of them carefully observed by mounted police officers. When the Carpathia was seen close to shore, ships' horns shouted in acknowledgement, but were nearly drowned by the roars of the crowd that had gathered, as everyone watched the boat of survivors rise up at the horizon.

The cheers were later immediately followed by the silent tears of those with an interest in the game, including family members of those who might or might be rescued from the sinking Titanic. The ship didn't immediately set off for the Cunard Pier but instead, it veered off and approached White Star Pier. White Star Pier. There, the crowd was with awe as the lifeboats of the Titanic were lifted up from the Carpathia and then sent to slowly glide towards to the White Star Line Pier.

It was a fitting thing for the sunken ship of the White Star Line, to be able to have the only thing that was left of it--its lifeboats--returned into its White Star Pier. After this poignant moment that the Carpathia returned to the Cunard dock, and stationed in the harbor, and began to load their human cargo.

When loved ones hugged their relatives who have passed away Joyful cries mixed with sadness were heard. For those who discovered their loved ones were not on the Carpathia was a torrent of complete grief and awe. It was the point of no return, during which the people who had to go on with the task of living, had to determine whether or not their beloved family members had made it through.

With the finality of the funeral in place whatever closure was left was offered to the grieving family was scheduled over the next weekend. The following weekend was full of funeral services. The pulpits were filled with sermons that sought to confront the events that had transpired. Naturally there were many sessions of "Nearer Thy God to Thee" that were played to the mourners. It was considered to be the last song that Titanic's onboard band sang before the waves took the ship away.

Following the incident there was no shortage of people trying to understand why the sinking of Titanic took place. It appears that a some of the process of closure required understanding the ways in which the captains of this vessel might have gone wrong. Humans generally search for someone to blame whenever catastrophes happen, and it wasn't long before criticisms to be hurled at the highest levels of leadership in the Titanic.

In many of funeral services following there were many speakers who took their message to a higher degree, even going as that they questioned the reason God would permit this kind of catastrophe to happen. The issue of why God is inherently good God allowed evil to exist to happen in the world is obviously, not something that was is just a thought to justify the

Titanic however, it is it has been discussed by theologians and philosophers alike.

In the event that one is convinced of the all-powerful, good, all-knowing God the simplest answer for the reason God isn't able to intervene in human affairs each and every moment that something happens would be absurd. Think about it. It is a time where we are free to exercise our choice. How would we live in if every time something negative happens, God comes down in heaven, intervening? It's not like the one we're familiar with.

If a throng of angels came down from the sky each time we stomped our toes, the Earth could be a complete mystery to us. Many theologians who preached about the subject at the burials of Titanic victims reminded audience to live in a flawed world where we all have the freedom to choose. The God of heaven did not intend to cause that the Titanic to sink however we are in a world of different choices we can freely make.

If a string of collective decisions (choices like the design of a ship that does not have sufficient lifeboats!) eventually lead to catastrophes such as the Titanic, then that's the kind of our world that we are living in. It's as simple as it gets (or according to the sermons during the Titanic tributes). This has nothing to be concerned with God's goodness. God. God's still good. are just living in a society that is the result of our own freewill and the choices we all must make. This was the general theme of of the sermons given at the numerous eulogies that were given to Titanic survivors.

However, there were those who could not help but feel guilt-ridden by the catastrophe and maybe even feel perhaps a bit guilt. Like the main engineer of the Titanic--Alexander Clarke--who was said to be overwhelmed during the funeral ceremony that was held in England and then fell unconscious right during the sermon, eventually losing consciousness before falling to the ground.

Although the events that caused the sinking the Titanic are complex however, the human mind cannot avoid looking for the source of blame. This was evident as the funeral services came to a end and the "letters of the editors" from various popular newspapers across the Atlantic were filled with all sorts of people expressing their views about the reasons what caused the sinking of the Titanic was averted.

It's sometimes remarkable how people who weren't even in the scene of a catastrophe feel they have the ability to comprehend the inner workings of the tragedy better than those who are intimately involved, however this is often the situation. One of the most illuminating chair quarterbacks of the day was a New York Herald's opinion column.

In the time period following the weekend when the rescue of the survivors when one Heraldcontributor said, "Had this latest expression of the mercantile naval construction equipped with fewer folderols, like swimming tanks, gymnasiums and other necessities to ensure the safety of sailors as well as life-rafts and more boats could have been carried, and each life could have been saved in the conditions which prevailed at the time the Titanic suffered her fatal blow."

There is perhaps something to the author said. Should the Titanic was filled with lifeboats, rather than lavish amenities one could argue said that more might have been saved. But , in the end the primary draw for Titanic was its luxury. Titanic was its luxury. It was a luxury liner in the end, was the main reason behind Titanic's its existence in the first place. This is why it was built.

It wasn't designed to be safe, it was constructed to treat its passengers with extravagant luxurious. In hindsight, always 20/20, it's hard to be blamed by the designers of the vessel to put their focus on luxury rather than security, when they were aware that building an elegant liner was exactly what their finance managers required them to do. However the accusations and guilt remained in the same place even following the loss of the vessel for many years to be.

How Do You Stay Alive?

"Then as we walked over the edge of the ocean we saw one light, then another beneath it. It appeared like it was too unbelievable to be real and I'm sure all eyes were filled with tears, both men's as well and women's. We were greeted with cheers and shouts."

Lawrence Beesley Titanic survivor

Since the sinking of the Titanic in the past, it's been discussed as to why it could be that certain people--like Molly Brown, who was aforementioned unsinkable capable of continuing their lives. Others were left hopelessly damaged and broken. Well, perhaps this is stating the obvious but, simply said--different people handle different things--well--differently.

It is believed that only the most determined of them who were able to swiftly recover from the Titanic tragedy, without suffering the lingering effects. Many would seek a middle ground, and time will certainly repair their injuries but, even then they wouldn't ever be the same. There were also those souls who were really broken by the tragedy or hid in a dark corner as a recluse or perhaps were even escorted into an insane institution-- these sad victims of the lingering trauma never fully recovered.

One of the most spirited and spirited survivors, but a bit sour of the Titanic was Renee Harris. She. Harris was a prominent New York socialite, the spouse of a theater guru before the tragedy on the Titanic. While she was able to survive her husband's loss, he was swept away along with the ship. At first, Renee was well taken well by her family due to investment options and stocks that the Mr. Harris had left her.

However, following the crash in stock markets in 1929 her fortunes began to slide. Also, she began having unresolved disputes with another survivor who was a British socialite Duff Gordon. Duff Gordon. Lady Duff. Gordon was fortunate enough to be able to survive with her husband, but instead of being content with her life she would in the future discredit the widows of the Titanic who weren't as fortunate.

Lady Duff Gordon wrote her memoirs a few years afterward, in 1932, and she decided to take aim at grieving women everywhere without any apparent reason, and sing out American women in particular. She wrote "Even during that harrowing moment I was awestruck at almost all American wives who had to leave their husbands, without a expression of regret or protest and with no words of goodbye. They've elevated the cult of chivalry up to levels in the United States that it's normal for their men to give up themselves and their wives to allow them to perform it."

When you consider the pain and suffering that was felt by the majority of people and enduring, the idea that American women would be happy to leave with their husbands was completely absurd. In fact, one American woman, specifically Renee Harris, was angry enough over the insults to write her own response. Her words were published in an article in Liberty Magazine. Renee Harris, replying to Lady Duff Gordon directly, wrote, "How dare you say this in a time when we all were devastated by the loss of our spouses. You're aware of how precious Harry is to me. I'll never be able to recover from his loss , which caused me to be financially ruined and devastated."

In spite of Lady Duff Gordon's claims that it was not difficult to American women to leave their partners, Renee Harris positioned herself as a living example of what the burden this separation was. For those who survived were also faced with the constant rehashing of the events that took place in the media. Additionally, there were a number of hearings in which survivors' stories were reviewed and reexamined as a desperate effort to give the public an answer to the constant question of what was wrong?

One of the people dragged out to be questioned was the one who first saw the glacier that eventually sank the Titanic Crewman Frederick Fleet. Frederick Fleet. Fleet was asked exactly what the iceberg appeared at the time he first saw it from the bird's nest. For the majority of people it appeared that the Titanic was a huge, half-sunken mountain. It was somewhat surprising so it was interesting to hear the testimony of Mr. Fleet testify that the Iceberg was not that huge when he first gazed at it.

For a better understanding his audience, he asked "Was it as big as an average house? Was it as big as it seems to be?" To which Mr. Fleet answered, "No No, no. It doesn't look very big in any way," before explaining, "it'd be the same size as the two tables when I first saw it." From an equidistant distance, it is evident that the iceberg which hit the Titanic initially appeared very tiny. Even after The Titanic struck the floating piece of ice, it looked small.

Based on Fleet, "When we were close by, it was just slightly higher than the head of the forecastle. It was about 50 feet, to be precise." From the distance, size can be deceiving and the first look of the object made him unable to grasp just how massive it was. However, when he was close enough to see the object, while the object appeared to be massive however, it didn't seem to rise before the crew as the size of a mountain.

According to Fleet it was able to rise over the forecastle, however it wasn't as massive as many people thought. The thing with icebergs is that the visible part is just the tip. In fact, as the well-known phrase states, that was just the top of the Iceberg. The majority of the floating mass of frozen ice was underneath the water and it was the ice beneath the water that cut across the sides of the Titanic and caused fatal injuries to the vessel.

One of the most important elements of Fleet's testimony was his admission that he wasn't provided with binoculars that were suitable. Fleet was forced to rely on his own eyesight to estimate the size and threat from the giant iceberg. Many believed they believed that White Star company was in the wrong for not providing crew members with binoculars , so that they could accurately evaluate potential dangers in the waters.

White Star of course denied any responsibility, saying that binoculars wouldn't be a factor on the day. At an investigation, it was found that the Titanic was struck by an fatal 300-foot cut to its lower side. And , despite efforts to close off the affected areas, the vessel was filling up with too much water too quickly.

While the initial phase of recovery was over, throughout the years, various parts from the boat, as well as human remains would be discovered from time-to-time.

The most valuable prize but the actual debris of the Titanic itself -- would remain hidden from the world until one particular day in the year 1985.

Chapter 11: Titanic Found At Long Last

"My mother was apprehensive right from the word "Go. She was aware that it was something that she had to be scared of and the one thing she was concerned about was to declare that an unsinkable ship was a blatant insult to the will of God. That was her words"

Eva Hart Titanic survivor

Before any thoughts of finding the wreck of the Titanic initially, the primary recovery efforts were focused on locating the bodies of the deceased. It was in 1912 shortly after the sinking that the first expeditions to retrieve bodies were launched. The company that had ordered the Titanic--White Star Line- made use of a ship which was from close to Halifax, Nova Scotia, in an effort to discover the bodies of the victims.

Other Canadian vessels were later called upon: the Algerine as well as the ship that supplied Montmagny as well as the cable vessel called Minia. All of these ships came with all the furniture of floating funeral homes, including embalming equipment, priests, morticians, and morticians.

It was deemed necessary to immediately embalm all bodies that were recovered prior to taking them back to dry ground, due to health reasons. In the event of a shortage in embalming liquid, however it led to the development of a cold calculation--recovery teams dumped the bodies of the poor people overboard to preserve the fluid used to embalm for more wealthy corpses to be that were retrieved.

It was considered appropriate in the moment because it was believed that the wealthier of the deceased were likely to have unresolved legal issues pertaining to their wills. It is beneficial to embalm them , and return them in order that things could be swiftly resolved. Many of us today are awestruck by this decision however, that was the feeling of the time.

The bodies which were considered worthy of embalming and resurrecting were transported to the nearest town to the place of rehabilitation--Halifax in Nova Scotia. In the end, around 333 bodies of the more than 1500 souls lost on the ship were found. What about how did they find the Titanic itself? The general location where the Titanic could be located was identified, since it was deep in the ocean that it would take a long time to actually send a crew down to find the Titanic's last remains.

It was on the 1st of September in 1985, an expedition jointly that was launched by France as well as the United States (led by Bob Ballard and Jean-Louis Michel) was able to dive deep enough to discover what was left from the Titanic. An underwater submersible named Argo was lowered to 12,400 feet below sea level. The underwater robot was able actually shine a spotlight on the darkness of the ocean and search for any trace of the long-forgotten Titanic.

All the underwater explorations were recorded on a waterproof camera and the blurry images was instantly transmitted back in the room of control on Argo's mothership the Knorr. With its vast coverage, Argo did not find the Titanic quickly but it would take some weeks of searching the deeps before the wreckage was found. While Titanic was Titanic seemed, it was the depressing vast, unending landscape of the ocean floor is a lot more and it took some time to pinpoint the exact location for the Titanic.

The first indication of the wreckage that the controllers of Argo found is the boiler of Titanic. The boiler was blowing prior to sinking, and then sank down to its bottom. The underwater cameras were now taking pictures of a perfect circular shape in the sea floor. This when examined closer, seemed as if it was the old boiler vessel. In the moments following the discovery that more images from the Titanic wreckage began to emerge.

Eyewitnesses have long claimed that the Titanic had broken into two pieces. This has been confirmed after the damaged bow as well as the stern which was destroyed by the Titanic were discovered wedged into the ocean floor, about 12,000 feet beneath the seafloor. The bow, which was smashed to pieces, was discovered in a different location.

The stories of survivors, noting that the vessel was split in two prior to sinking, were now almost certain. A study of the wreckage discovered that the vessel had split in two at the "low angle to the top" of the ocean and was just about to go under. This breaking in two that killed the rest of the passengers aboard the Titanic. If the ship hadn't been broken up like this it may be possible for some people to have made it long enough to make it to rescue.

Incredibly the physical evidence could support a theory which was quietly aired into 1912, shortly after the sinking. In the course of the numerous inquests and hearings that were held, it was thought that the shipbuilders of the luxurious liner made an effort for savings and created a slack in the process of construction by failing to properly reinforce the hull. The subsequent investigation of the underwater wreckage may lend support to this theory of malfeasance on the part of shipbuilders.

The depth beneath the ocean, the force exerted by the water is believed to be more than six hundred pounds for every square inch. The two parts of the Titanic were laid on the ocean floor about 1/3 of a mile from each otherand far from the shores in Newfoundland. Canadian province, Newfoundland. Incredibly, this place is 13.2 miles from the last coordinates that were read by the Titanic's slain radio operator.

It is believed that radio operators mistakenly guessed in the logical confusion caused by that sinking Titanic. There is also the possibility that the remains of the vessel drifted off into the sea later. When the wreckage was discovered it was discovered that both halves of the Titanic had to have struck deep into the water with tremendous force. It was massive in fact, it caused the bow of the ship to be smashed, and the stern to become nearly inaccessible.

Only the bow which remained mostly in good condition. It is believed that the strength for the stern had been damaged when the ship sank, and this structural flaw caused the stern to break and collapse when it struck the sea floor. Both sides of the Titanic are, in the meantime are enclosed by a large "debris fields" filled with wreckage. In this wreckage are some of the victims who were left who were buried for a long time in the sea.

Conclusion

Following the sinking Titanic numerous inquiries and hearings into the tragedy resulted in the conclusion that, from both sides of Atlantic that the most significant mistake in the sinking of Titanic was that enough lifeboats were not equipped. Although some may believe it was hundreds of men to be killed with shouts of "Women and children first!" !"--it could have been prevented.

If there were only an abundance of lifeboats, all the widowed and orphaned children would not have lost their parents and husbands. It was because of the needless death that rules were enacted and made it a regular procedure for all vessels operating on waterways to provide life-saving, emergency vessels for everyone who is on board.

The recommendations were codified into legislation, following the adoption of the "International Convention for the Protection of Life at the Sea" that was signed in 1914. These protocols have undergone several modifications, and a second version of this was enacted in 1974.

The tragic tale of the Titanic was not a disaster that should have occurred. In the wake of this terrible maritime accident in the context of how the ship sank Titanic it will forever be the selfless sacrifices that the people who put their lives at risk to save others . Their sacrifice will never cease to be remembered.

www.ingramcontent.com/pod-product-compliance
Lightning Source LLC
Chambersburg PA
CBHW050025130526
44590CB00042B/1914